Robin McGibbon has ghost-written two ~~and My Brothers~~ for Charles Kray and *For Ever and Ever, Eamonn* for the late broadcaster's widow, Grainne Andrews. He lives in Kent with his second wife, Sue, and has four children by his previous marriage.

Robin McGibbon played senior amateur soccer for many years but his one proud claim to football fame is that the legendary Newcastle United hero Jackie Milburn asked him to substitute for him – and play alongside Tom Finney – in a star-studded representative match in Italy in 1973.

GAZZA!

A Biography

Robin McGibbon

PENGUIN BOOKS

PENGUIN BOOKS

Published by the Penguin Group
Penguin Books Ltd, 27 Wrights Lane, London w8 5tz, England
Viking Penguin, a division of Penguin Books USA Inc.
375 Hudson Street, New York, New York, 10014, USA
Penguin Books, Australia Ltd, Ringwood, Victoria, Australia
Penguin Books Canada Ltd, 2801 John Street, Markham, Ontario, Canada l3r 1b4
Penguin Books (NZ) Ltd, 182–190 Wairau Road, Auckland 10, New Zealand

Penguin Books Ltd, Registered Offices: Harmondsworth, Middlesex, England

First published 1990
1 3 5 7 9 10 8 6 4 2

Copyright © Robin McGibbon, 1990
All rights reserved

The moral right of the author has been asserted

Printed in England by Clays Ltd, St Ives plc
Filmset in Plantin

For Elizabeth Tompsett,

a bunch of green bananas,
for your unfaltering support
and bright outlook in our dark times.

MY THANKS

Many people were generous with their time helping with this tribute, but I would like to thank certain individuals without whom the book would not have been possible.

In no particular order, I must thank all of Paul's schoolteachers for their fascinating memories; the kind gentlemen at Redheugh Boys' Club, Evan Bryson, Tommy Leonard and Terry Ritson, who remembered the lovable rascal; scouts Brian Clark and Peter Kirkley, for recalling the exciting talent; Colin Suggett for having second thoughts; Margaret, Maureen and Madeline for giving me a giggle; Willie McFaul for his openness; John Pickering for his patience; Tony Towerd for the vital statistics; Alistair Garvie for filling in a gap; and, also on Tyneside, all the helpful girls at the Springfield Hotel, the Tyne and Wear Archives Service and John Deacon at Tyne Tees Television, who snipped the red tape.

I'm grateful to Bobby Robson for not letting me down; to Dave Sexton, Don Howe, Mike Kelly and Tony Dorigo for setting the international scene; and to Vinny Jones for playing ball. Thanks should also go to Peter Shilton and Kenny Sansom, whose contributions didn't make the finished product but are appreciated nevertheless.

On the personal side, I would thank Steven Taylor and David Billing for staying on-side, Mickey Moynihan for always being there, and my wife, Sue, for far, far more than all those uncomplaining hours at the WP.

Above all, I would like to thank my son, Robin, who had the idea for the book, and worked tirelessly with me to make sure it was written.

Robin McGibbon

I

Jean Bell was preparing breakfast that frosty Christmas morning when she heard a child playing outside. She went to a front window and looked out on to Edison Gardens; it was quiet and deserted, except for a tubby little boy in a brown knitted pullover, jeans and hard black shoes, playing with a black and white plastic football. She smiled to herself: she was so happy for him. He had got his present after all – got the football he'd been talking about all those exciting weeks leading up to Christmas. Jean was thrilled for him. His mother had told her two months before that with her husband not working, money was tight; that it was touch and go whether the boy and his sister and brother would get what they wanted for Christmas.

Later that morning, Jean opened her front door to get the milk off the doorstep. Seeing her, the boy picked up his ball and ran quickly to her front gate.

'Look what Father Christmas brought me,' he said, smiling, proudly showing her the ball.

'Aren't you lucky?' Jean said. But the boy was not listening: he was sprinting into his own house next door. Seconds later he ran out, holding up a pair of tiny football boots.

'Father Christmas brought me these, too,' he said, breathless with excitement.

'You *are* a lucky boy, aren't you?' Jean said. Still smiling, she watched him run off and start kicking the ball along the street again.

At lunchtime, Jean heard the boy's mother calling him in. But he didn't seem to hear; didn't want to. She called twice more, but a small voice just called out: 'In a minute, mam, I'm playing.' And the sound of the ball bouncing on concrete filled the quiet afternoon air.

Again, the mother's loud voice. 'Come in. Your dinner's on the table.'

No reply. Just the sound of the ball and the boy chasing it.

'Come in. *Now*.'

'Just coming, mam,' the boy shouted, his eyes still on the ball.

A couple of minutes and more calls later, the mother's patience snapped. She strode impatiently up the path and into the street. She grabbed her son by the shoulders. 'Get inside. NOW.'

Reluctantly, the little boy picked up his ball and marched forlornly ahead of his mother into the house for his Christmas dinner.

Less than an hour later he was out again, kicking the ball from one side of the street to the other, dribbling it down the middle or stopping to kick it out of his hands into the air. He was happy in a world of his own and he played with that ball all afternoon until dusk draped the rows of red-brick semis and his mother called him in for tea.

The boy was out early the next day, too. And the next. And the next. He and the ball were inseparable and he played with it for hours, in rain and wind, even snow. It was like a playmate. He didn't need anyone or anything else.

For four-year-old Paul Gascoigne the ball that Santa brought him that Christmas of 1971 was the best present he could have wished for and he took it everywhere – even to bed.

The neighbours in Edison Gardens may have been surprised at Paul's obsession, but his parents, John and Carol Gascoigne, were not. They were aware of it shortly after he was born, on 27 May 1967, two miles away in Teams, a shabby, poverty-stricken area of Gateshead, on the banks of the River Tyne.

There were just sixteen cramped rented flats in four

8

large houses in Pitt Street, and the Gascoignes lived in one, on the first floor, at number 29, just down the cobblestoned street from number 33, where John's parents had a first-floor flat. Unemployment in the area was high, and, with no trade, John found it harder than most to get a job. Carol was more than willing to work, but in the late sixties she had her hands full with three young children – Paul, his elder sister, Anna, and younger brother, Carl. For most of the time, the family struggled along on what they could scrape together.

With parents finding it hard to cope with their own problems, Paul was left to find his own amusement. And he did – with a ball. He swung his first kick at just nine months and was kicking a ball against his front garden wall at the age of two.

The bug had certainly bitten, because over the next two years Paul was never happy unless he had a ball at his feet. Even mealtimes were an intrusion into his playtime, and it was common for him to kick a ball around on Pitt Street's cobblestones while holding a slice of bread and margarine he'd been too impatient to finish at the table.

The Gascoignes moved on to better, slightly more spacious, accommodation in Oak and Pine Streets, but Pitt Street was close, and Carol made sure the children saw a lot of their grandparents. Paul would love showing off his growing football skills to his grandad. He would dribble a ball down the dead-end street, calling out proudly: 'Look, grandad, I'm just like Georgie Best.'

With money desperately tight, Carol could not afford such a luxury as a new ball, so Paul made do with whatever he could find. It did not matter whether it was a worn plastic ball, barely full of air, or a threadbare tennis ball: he would spend hours, often alone, just kicking it against his front garden wall or across the cobblestones to the high wall of the old Rose Street Junior School.

By the time his family moved to Edison Gardens, in Bensham, and he was given that first full-size football for

Christmas, Paul was eager to teach himself skills, and he would dribble round lamp-posts, or simply swerve round imaginary opponents, always taking care to keep his new ball under control. As he got older, he would lay tin cans and large stones in a line on the pavement and practise dribbling in between them. At seven, his touch had improved so much he taught himself to keep the ball up in the air. That ball, it seemed, was like an extension of his right foot and he hated going anywhere without it. Whenever his mother or neighbours asked him to run an errand – or message, as they say in the North East – the first thing he'd ask, in broad Geordie, was, 'Cannah I take ma ball?' And then off he'd go to the shops, dribbling his ball round whatever, or whoever, got in the way.

'He was football daft, all right,' Jean Bell remembers. 'He'd come home from school, grab a biscuit or a sandwich to keep him going till tea, then take a ball into the street and start practising his skills. Sometimes another kid would join in, but most of the time Paul would kick around on his own. It didn't matter what the weather was like. Once, I saw him out there all alone, trying to kick his ball through thick snow.

'He would be in a world of his own – just him and a ball – and he never wanted to leave it.

'When he did go in for his tea, I was told he would sit at the table with his feet on the ball, scoffing his food in a hurry so that he could go out again. As soon as the last mouthful was almost gone, he'd jump up and say, "Right, mam – I'm going out." I found it fascinating watching him. He was so good.

'I knew he wanted a full-size ball – and boots – that Christmas, but Carol had told me she didn't think she could afford them.

'I just said, "You'll get them, don't worry." I believed it. Paul wanted them so badly, I just knew she wouldn't disappoint him. I haven't a clue how she managed, because her husband wasn't working and they had very little money.

But Paul got his boots and ball and the other kids got presents, too.

'Unlike his younger brother, Carl, Paul was quiet and reserved. Carl would back-answer you cheekily, but Paul was more polite. If you told him off, he'd speak up for himself, but was never nasty. If he was in the wrong, he'd always say, "Sorry, Mrs Bell."

'If someone kicked the ball into our back garden, the other boys would climb over and get it, but Paul would always come to the front door and ask me if I would get it – even though I had a mongrel dog and Paul was terrified of it. He'd knock at the door, then run back down the path to the gate and say from a safe distance, "Please, Mrs Bell, could I have ma ball back, please?" He was a nice kid.'

The teachers at nearby Brighton Avenue Junior School thought so, too. Paul was a chirpy little boy with a bubbly personality, and very pleasant and cooperative, although his work was rather untidy and below the average of his seven-year-old classmates.

The teachers quickly learned, however, that if Paul Gascoigne did not have much in his head, he certainly had more than enough in his feet. Even at seven, he was so much better at football than other boys and would try to organize players in their school-yard matches.

Peter Savage, who taught Paul and took all sports lessons, says today: 'I first saw him playing in the yard during morning break. He was dynamite. The ball seemed to be glued to his foot. He would just cruise round other boys and the only way they could get the ball off him was to crowd him out. He lived for football even then and would play whenever he could – before school, during playtimes and in the lunch break. They were typical schoolboy games, with a couple of bags for goalposts and anything from five each side to fifteen. Paul was so much more aware than the other boys and would get so frustrated if things did not go right that he would get the ball and take on the whole opposition himself. It was real Roy of the Rovers stuff – even at seven.'

There is no evidence that Paul skipped lessons to play with a ball, but he did not always make it in time to answer his name at assembly. When there was no answer, the headmaster would say: 'Paul Gascoigne – out here NOW!' Then he would ask if anyone knew where Paul was, or if he was ill. No one told tales, but most of his class knew he was kicking a ball around in the covered area of the school yard, using the huge stone pillars as goalposts.

Mr Savage knew Paul had an exceptional talent for the school team, but boys were not selected until they were nine or ten, and, in spite of his skill, Paul was too young. That did not stop him from continually asking for a game, however – particularly if he saw on the school notice-board that the team was not winning!

In September, four months after Paul's eighth birthday, that notice-board informed boys that trials were to be held for the football team. No signatures were needed. Boys interested just had to be at the school the following Friday to meet a single-decker bus that would take them to the Shuttles, the school playing fields in Eslington Park, a mile away.

Paul was one of the first to arrive. And although he was at least a year younger than other likely contenders, Mr Savage was so impressed with his play that he felt compelled to give him a chance.

'It was the remarkable *individual* talent that first appealed to me, but then I saw his ability to play in a team,' says Mr Savage. 'Sydney Millen, the headmaster, and I were worried Paul might get a big head, so we played his talent down. We never went overboard in our praise, and I didn't select him for every game. I knew he would be in the team all the time in his third and fourth years and I wanted to give less-talented older boys a chance. Paul is the only boy to play for the school at the age of eight, as far as I know.'

Paul became a school-team regular the following year. He could hit the ball well with either foot and it would take so many players to crowd him out that his teacher nicknamed him 'steam engine'.

'Once he got into gear, I always thought it would take a brick wall to stop him,' says Mr Savage. 'He would play so long with the team, but if we went a goal or two down, he'd go back deep into his own half, pick up the ball, then go straight at the opposition on his own. Once, he went by players in a forty- or fifty-yard run – and just when everyone thought he was going to pass, he let go with a cracking shot from outside the penalty area. It hit the bar with such force I thought it was going to snap.'

The more Paul shone in those matches, the more he was talked about at other schools, and rival teams would usually put their best player on him to try to mark him out of the game. Such was Paul's ingenuity, that it usually took *three* players to stop him!

'He was so unpredictable and had the ability to produce a goal out of nothing,' says Mr Savage. 'You could sense the excitement of kids watching from the line. They'd seem to hold their breath in anticipation every time he picked up a pass. They'd nudge each other, excitedly, and say, "Gascoigne's got the ball!" Crunch games always centred around Paul. When he was in possession, there was always panic in the opposition.'

No game was more of a crunch than when Brighton Avenue played St Cuthbert's. They were always close games, with St Cuthbert's having the edge, thanks to a strong, powerfully built boy, who was the only one on the Gateshead school scene to rival Paul in ability; indeed, most people thought he was even better than Paul and destined to become a professional footballer. The boy's name was Keith Spraggon and he and Paul had a sneaking regard for each other, in a young schoolboy way.

Brighton Avenue never won any competitions among the six schools in the league, and it upset Paul. His will to win was strong even then, and, when the team had come close, he would troop off towards an old shed used for changing rooms, in tears.

'He was an emotional lad,' says Mr Savage. 'Whatever he was feeling showed in his face.'

The tears never lasted long, though. Paul was a cheery lad, who lived for football, and no sooner had one match finished than he was looking forward eagerly to the next.

Talk to anyone who knew Paul in those days and they will all say that, as far as football was concerned, he had always been ahead of his years. And it was not surprising that he soon began to want, need, the challenge of older boys. At eight, he thought nothing of playing with twelve, even thirteen-year-olds.

One of them was Paul Thompson, who in the early seventies ran an Edison Gardens team in an unofficial street league.

Mr Thompson, now a Gateshead taxi driver, said, 'Not many eight-year-olds would want to play against boys so much older, but Paul loved it. He was never in awe of anyone and I never once saw him intimidated.

'You would understand a smaller boy getting rid of the ball quickly to avoid being tackled, but Paul was not afraid to run at players, take them on, and go for goal. Being tubby, he was never a fast player; he relied on his ball control, dribbling and dummying skills, and fantastic passing ability. And he seemed to have a fixation about the ball; he never took his eyes off it. When he was playing, I'm sure he was blind to any traffic, because he was so intent on watching the ball.

'Everyone was surprised at how much ability Paul had for someone so small and young. There's no doubt that playing with older, bigger and stronger boys helped him improve.

'We used to play a game where we had to defend different garden gates up and down the street. We kicked up a racket and were always being chased by neighbours, angry at the ball crashing into their gates all the time. One woman, Dolly Smith, was after us all the time; if the ball ever landed in her garden we'd as good as lost it. It was nearly always Paul's ball we played with, and, once, Dolly said she was keeping it for two days to teach him a lesson. Paul could not have lasted two days without a ball, so he immediately borrowed one and the "Gates" game started all over again.

'Dolly and Paul liked each other, though. She was a passionate Newcastle supporter and would encourage him and his love of the game. One birthday or Christmas, Paul was given a black and white Newcastle shirt as a present and he always wore it over his jeans. In the summer, we'd play in that street and Paul never wanted to go in. His older sister would come out and tell him it was time to go in, but Paul never took any notice. Then his mother would call him. He'd shout out, "Five minutes, mam," and carry on playing. In the end, she would have to come out at about nine o'clock and tell him she would take his ball away if he didn't go in. That did the trick. Paul would never risk losing his ball.'

Paul's mother now had her hands even more full with a fourth addition to the family – a daughter named Lindsay – and Paul would spend more time at his grandparents' home in Teams. He loved it there. He had become friends with most of the boys in Pitt Street and many from Orton and Morrisson, two other tiny streets leading off Rose Street; and he revelled in regular football matches that were rarely less than fifteen a side, and sometimes more.

Pitt Street was less than fifty yards long and so narrow that two cars could not pass. There were houses on only one side, and they faced a high school wall that ran the length of the street. At the end, the wall joined a wooden fence which blocked off a grimy, ash-covered area that had once been a coal pit. Pitt Street was hardly an ideal soccer pitch: apart from the uneven cobbles that made ball control difficult, the teams had to play partly across the street, not straight down it. Two posts and a crossbar were marked out on the fence at the pit end, but the other goal was a space between a gas lamp on a footpath opposite the houses, and a line chalked on the school wall. This meant the team defending the pit dead-end had to turn a sharp left to score into the gas lamp goal. Someone, it seems, felt it wise not to have a goal at the opposite end of the street because the ball would have kept rolling into Rose Street, which might be busy with traffic. To make the game more difficult, the balls the boys played with were often only half filled with air; indeed, sometimes nobody had a football at all and they played with a worn tennis ball. It was worth a boy making the effort to find a ball, because it would give him the right to captain one of the teams and pick the players he wanted.

Paul often brought a ball to those matches; but even if he didn't, he still captained the other team and generally organized the game, which had 'home-made' rules such as: three corners earn a penalty; and anyone scoring three times goes in goal.

Neither the uneven surface, strangely positioned goal, nor the deflated balls bothered Paul. His enthusiasm was as fierce as ever and, if anything, the hazards helped him improve his skills because he had to try that bit harder to make things work. And his desire to win was so strong, he would make sure he had the better players.

If Paul was unhappy that his father was not living with his mother all the time, he did not show it. There was, after all, a lot to occupy him in his after-school hours near his grandparents' home: the disused pit provided an ex-hilarating course for daring rides, and Paul would love hurtling down the long bumpy slope in a home-made bogey (go-cart), or on the handlebars of a junk-yard bike with no pedals or saddle. When he was not there, or not kicking a ball, he would be with other boys, collecting lemonade bottles for refunds, or newspapers, which the local fish-and-chip shop across the old pit exchanged for chips. For most children in the Teams area, fish itself was a luxury. Families would be so hard up that mothers would make meals from off-cuts they bought at the butcher's at a third of the price; a tasty favourite that went a long way was potatoes sliced with stock and tomatoes and bacon pieces. Ham bones were used for soup, and bread was usually spread with dripping or margarine. With money so hard to come by, making a penny or two in whatever way they could was a way of life for youngsters in Teams.

With wholesome food so hard to afford, it is difficult to understand why Paul was on the tubby side. He was a hyperactive boy, always burning off energy, and one would have thought he'd be the last to carry surplus weight, even puppy fat.

But he did have a weakness for sweets and chocolate; and what pennies he did earn were spent in a shop on the corner of Pitt and Rose Streets, run by an old spinster called Lily. She always had her hair tied back in a bun and looked like a strait-laced 'schoolmarm', but the children adored her; her converted house stocked all they could possibly want and she knew where everything was. For Paul, it was an Aladdin's Cave and it drew him like a magnet – just like the Redheugh Boys' Club, which was held in an old school building on the other side of the wall in Pitt Street.

When he was six and seven years old, he had watched in awe, as dozens of bigger boys turned up every night and kicked a football around the Rose Street school yard, waiting for the doors of the old school to open at seven o'clock. He did not know what was behind those doors, what the boys did when they went inside. But they were all laughing and joking and enjoying themselves, and Paul liked the feel of it; to a boy with not the most settled home life, it was a magical gathering and he wished he was older and able to be part of it.

Now, at eight, the lure of that club was even stronger.

The desire to be part of a group, in a warm, happy atmosphere, was still there. But now there was something else: the football. He'd still watch the early arrivals kicking around in the school yard; but, with his growing confidence, he now watched not so much in awe but in envy. How he longed to join in! How he wished he could show those older boys the tricks he had taught himself. He watched, transfixed, from the sidelines, willing the ball to go out of play so that he could fetch it. When it did, Paul would run and turn with it – perhaps flicking it up deftly – before knocking it back with accuracy and not a little power.

He knew he was good and could hold his own with older boys. And it is possible, when they saw those brief flashes of skill, that the thirteen-year-old veterans of Redheugh Boys' Club knew it, too.

Sadly, however, the club rules stated that the minimum joining age was ten: Paul had two years to wait.

Two years. It might as well be twenty! He did not want to wait that long. He wanted to be ten today. He wanted to get into that club and show them what he could do with a football, perhaps get in one of the teams that played in a league. He was only eight, but he was playing in his school team sometimes. Why could he not be in that club *now*?

Night after night, week after week, he hung around outside the club, watching the football, listening to the laughter, wishing his life away. He would tell his grandad how much he wanted to join the club. And whenever he saw his dad, he told him, too.

The only thing the tubby little boy wanted out of life, it seemed, was to walk through the doors of Redheugh Boys' Club as an official member.

And then one September night in 1975, his father took him along to meet Tommy Leonard, who'd been running the club for seventeen years.

And what Tommy said made it the happiest night of Paul Gascoigne's eight-year-old life.

2

Tommy Leonard knew Paul. He'd lived in one of the sixteen flats in Pitt Street and seen the lad grow up. He had watched him as a toddler, kicking a ball against his garden wall in his black plimsolls. He'd watched him a couple of years later, playing football in the street and running rings round older boys in a couple of school games. He'd seen him kicking a tin can around while other boys were playing in the dirt of the old pit area. He'd also seen him hanging around the school on club nights, anxious for a kick of the older boys' ball. Tommy knew Paul was a pretty useful little footballer all right.

He also knew full well that he wasn't ten, which made it rather awkward that night when Paul's father took his son to the converted Rose Street school and insisted he was.

'I decided to turn a blind eye,' Tommy remembers. 'I couldn't turn the boy away. I couldn't turn any boy away; Teams was a rough old area and there was nowhere else for kids to go. And Paul was so keen. He genuinely wanted to come into the club to take part, not like many other kids who just wanted to get out of the rain. So I said yes, Paul could join as an associate member. But I made it clear that meant he could only use the club's facilities, not play in organized team football matches.

'Then I looked down at Paul seriously and warned: "You had better behave yourself, lad."

'Paul looked up at me, with a cheeky look I'd seen in the street and outside the club many times before: "Thank you, Mr Leonard. I will," he said.'

Tommy and another club official, Evan Bryson, then took John Gascoigne and Paul round the old school building, which had been converted into the club's new premises in 1969. Rooms leading off what was once the small assembly hall now held snooker and table-tennis tables. One room in particular that caught Paul's eye was filled with football trophies, for Redheugh had a reputation for breeding successful teams and had won dozens of competitions since it was started in 1957. Paul stood staring at the cups and shields, deep in thought, then Tommy and Evan took him to the door at the front of the club, overlooking the school yard.

The Under-14 coach, Denis Washbourne, who was training a bunch of lads at the time, remembers the evening vividly, because Paul's football reputation had gone before him.

'I knew who he was because Tommy Leonard had seen him play for his school against St Cuthbert's and had told me what a great player he was,' says Denis. 'I remember Paul standing at the top of the stone steps outside the club that evening in a light grey V-neck jumper, dark trousers and black trainers, watching the lads train in the yard. Evan had a hand on his shoulder and was telling him about the club and the teams we ran, but Paul was just staring at the boys training as though transfixed.'

After that first meeting, Paul was at the club virtually every night; his father would walk him there from Edison Gardens and have a drink with some pals in a pub, while Paul played in the club. If the boy was embarrassed that he was often the last one in the club because his father was late picking him up, he certainly did not show it.

'We'd stay with Paul until his dad arrived and he would be quite content, chatting away to us,' says Denis. 'He was a bouncy kid, always cheerful, and he was happy to stay in the club as long as he could. He'd be there until 10.30 p.m. some nights and, if his father wasn't picking him up, Evan would drop him home in the van.

'Paul spent a lot of time on his own away from his family. The only friends he seemed to have were the boys in the club.'

Paul may have been too young to play for Redheugh, but that did not mean he was not allowed to *watch* club matches. He was so keen he would go wherever the Under-18 team were playing – even on his own.

'No matter what the weather, Paul would be there,' says Denis. 'He'd be there every week, kicking one of the spare balls into the back of the net, one eye on the ball, the other on the game. Sometimes other boys would be with him, but he was often there on his own, just kicking and watching.

'When the ball ran out of play, he was always the first to run after it, sometimes kicking it up in the air and trapping it before kicking it back, just to show what he could do.

'He was a willing helper, too, always first to help with the goal nets. To save us getting a pole, he'd offer to get on someone's shoulders and hook the nets to the posts and bar. After the game, he'd be there again to get them down, and then he'd race round the pitch gathering the corner flags. He was amazingly keen to do anything connected with football.

'One Saturday, though, he got hurt playing behind the goal. His training shoes were so thin, a curved piece of glass cut into the arch of his left foot as he went to kick the ball.

'One of the other lads told me and I raced over. Paul was lying on the ground, his injured foot crossed over the other to keep it off the ground, still watching the game and joking with his pals.

'It was such a nasty cut I didn't know what to do for the best. Finally, I carried Paul back to the halfway line where I had the first aid box. I told him I was going to pull the glass out and clean the wound. Paul just said. "Okay, then." He was still watching the game.

'I pulled out the glass in one piece and bandaged the foot. Then, with a quick thank you, Paul put on his sock and training shoe and quickly limped off, calling to one of his pals behind the goal to pass him the ball.'

*

Most new members were quiet and inhibited when they joined the club; they would stick close to the walls, watching what was going on, too shy yet to take part. But Paul's bubbly and charismatic personality quickly burst through and he was soon in the thick of things. He was a very popular boy, always with plenty to say for himself, and if a particular group had a point to make they were always happy for Paul to make it for them.

Every boy in the club quickly got a nickname. Some were not complimentary, such as Snotty, Mucky or Stinker. In one early rough and tumble, someone abbreviated Paul's unusual surname to a simple 'Gazza'. And that's what they called him in the club from that day on.

To Tommy Leonard, the Redheugh Boys' Club was a saviour for Paul. It was a warm and safe oasis amid the dirt and grime and toughness of a hard, working-class area; a haven that eased the pain of what loneliness he may have felt at having such an unsettled home life.

Had it not been for the club, Tommy is convinced Paul may have gone off the rails; perhaps been tempted by boredom to get involved in undesirable company and land in trouble. As it was, the boy threw himself into the activities of the club every night and was a picture of happiness. The only words from Tommy Leonard that would have made him happier were: 'You're in the football team.'

But the club's youngest side was for Under-14s. And now, at ten, it did not matter how skilful or keen Paul was, he was far too small.

He revelled in having somewhere to go, in being part of a young community, however, and he was always first in the school playground, waiting for Tommy Leonard or another club official to open up. All the hours, days, weeks of having to find his own amusement were over and he could not wait to get inside the club and get involved.

He had another good reason to be early. He and the other younger members played a football game called

'Doors' and it was a case of first-come-first-play. The game was just like 'Gates', which he had played in Edison Gardens, except that now the goals were the closed doors of rooms leading off the assembly hall. Only eight boys could play at a time, and they each picked a door, which they had to defend against the rest. When a player conceded three goals, he was out, and had to make way for another boy waiting on the sidelines. Naturally, the longer a boy made his three 'lives' last, the longer he played.

From the moment he joined the club, Paul was always one of the first in the hall to claim his favourite door – the one in the far left-hand corner from the entrance. It was in those frenetic free-for-all games that he was able to show off his skills. In such a confined space – roughly twenty yards by sixteen – with seven other boys trying to win the ball, one needed close control and good dribbling ability, and all his hours of practice had given Paul both. His tubbiness did not matter; the playing area was so small he did not have to run far, only twist and turn and keep the ball away from other players, which he did exceptionally well. Even then, he showed a fierce determination to win, and if he conceded a couple of goals he would run about like a terrier, desperate to keep his goal 'alive'. What let him down was his lack of height: while taller boys were able to head away high shots, Paul could not. He lost a lot of 'lives' that way.

Generally, though, Paul shone brightly. And his keenness and will to win, as much as his skill, told Tommy Leonard that, possibly, he was a Redheugh star of the future.

Certainly Peter Savage, Paul's teacher at Brighton Avenue, had no doubts about the boy's ability, and singled him out as the only boy from the school to go for a trial for Gateshead Boys Under-11s.

Although he was smaller and slower than the rest of the fifty boys from West Gateshead, Paul was one of the first to be picked out by Alan Egdell, who ran the town team.

Over the next two weeks, Paul shone in more trials,

23

involving boys from East and Central Gateshead, and was chosen to go for a coaching weekend at Dukeshousewood, a football camp in the country.

Another boy who made it to the camp was Paul's rival from St Cuthbert's – Keith Spraggon. It was the beginning of a strong friendship on the field – and at Redheugh Boys' Club.

Playing for Gateshead Boys, Paul picked up another nickname: 'Bamber', after TV's *University Challenge* quizmaster, Bamber Gascoigne.

Paul didn't know who he was at first, but when someone told him, he was quite flattered and liked it.

Paul had always been mischievous. Many times Tommy Leonard had watched him slyly widen the coats the older boys were using as goals in the yard, or kick away a tin can they had put down in the street to serve as 'Home' in a game of hide-and-seek.

As his confidence grew at Redheugh, this impish side of his nature grew and it would drive Tommy and his colleagues mad.

'He was a little urchin,' says Tommy. 'Mischief was his middle name. He was a Just William character, always up to some devilment or other. But he wasn't a nasty lad. His pranks were never malicious – just harmless fun, if a little irritating to myself and other club officials. He was a lovable little rogue – so cheeky, but you couldn't help liking him. Even if he'd been naughty you couldn't really fall out with him.

'Paul had a thing about not owning up. Never once would he admit he had done anything wrong – even if he'd been caught red-handed. I remember shouting at him dozens of times, "Right, once more and you're out that door." But he'd just look at me, in wide-eyed innocence, and say sweetly, "It wasn't me, Mr Leonard."

'He was a respectful boy. He never misbehaved if club officials were around, but the minute our backs were turned he'd be thinking what he could get up to.'

The club rules stated that the full-size snooker table was out of bounds to under-12s. But in those days the room was tucked away in a corner and difficult for organizers to monitor; some of the younger members would sneak in there when no one was looking and play on the table.

Evan remembers: 'The little 'uns would be devilish, and when I, or someone else, went in to check on things, a little crowd would scatter away from the table fast. When I asked what had been happening, they all looked a picture of innocence. I knew that someone got on the table and played "football" with the snooker balls because there would be footprints on the table and rips in the cloth, but no one ever owned up or told tales.

'I never actually caught Paul for anything in that snooker room, but I was pretty sure he was involved. Whenever I confronted him, he'd just give a cheeky grin and say, "It wasn't me, Mr Bryson." Later, we had to have the table moved from the room and repaired.'

Paul would do anything he thought would raise a laugh or cause a bit of excitement. He'd turn off the lights, tie other boys' shoe laces together, jog an older boy's arm as he lined up a snooker shot, or take the white ball off the table when the players were not looking. He would even place a plastic cup of water on the door so that one of the officials got a soaking.

One of his favourite pranks was to hide another boy's football shorts before he went out to play in the yard, which meant the boy would be last out of the changing rooms and have to run round the school building as a punishment.

'He had an impish sense of fun and so much zest,' says Tommy Leonard. 'To him, life was a bowl of cherries. I remember thinking how I wouldn't have liked the job of entertaining him at home. With all that energy, he wouldn't have been happy just sitting down quietly and reading a book.'

It was a sentiment Paul's teachers at Brighton Avenue

would have understood more than most. Throughout his four years there, it had been a constant battle trying to persuade him that life could not revolve around football *all* the time, that he needed to work hard at his studies, too.

'He was a trier at any subject, but a lot of hard work was required and he wasn't interested in anything but football,' says Peter Savage. 'I learned very early on that I could use it as a threat to good advantage. If he was misbehaving, I would only have to say, "No football for you, young man," and he would quieten down immediately.'

When he left Brighton Avenue, in the summer of 1978, Paul showed a thoughtful side of his nature when he bought Mr Savage a small brown novelty glass as a farewell and 'Thank You' present.

Paul, too, had something to remember the school by: a football trophy. He had been sponsored to take twelve penalties at three different goalkeepers to help raise funds for the Gateshead Primary Schools' Association and had scored every one. Mr Savage remembers how proud Paul was on the way home to Edison Gardens. It was the first trophy he had won, and that night he slept with it under his pillow.

Now eleven, Paul moved on to Breckenbeds Junior High, a mixed school in Saltwell Road, Low Fell, with about 750 pupils. One lunchtime, early in the term, teachers George Stephenson and Frank McGarry held a trial to see who would be candidates for the school football team. They sorted out between fifty and sixty boys into teams, then stood on a raised bank overlooking the pitches to watch them play.

It took the teachers just a few minutes to appreciate that one of the boys – a tubby little fellow, much smaller than everyone else – was quite outstanding.

'From the very start of the game you could see that the boy was the best player of the lot,' McGarry remembers. 'He had amazing ball control and vision for someone so young. When he had the ball, things really happened.

'After a few minutes, George and I turned to each other and said jointly, "He's in." We were delighted to have such a good player at the school. We didn't know his name at that stage, so we made a mental note of what he looked like. He was wearing a Newcastle strip, but many others were, too, so the main thing we remembered was his size. He was so tiny.

'When the games were over, I went to the changing room to find out his name. I had trouble finding him because he was so small, but when I did, I gave him the good news. He didn't react much, just said, "Thank you, sir," or something. That was my first meeting with Paul Gascoigne.

'In matches, he would line up at right midfield, but, once the whistle blew, he was all over the pitch, taking throw-ins, and even goal-kicks. He loved having the ball at his feet, and when he passed the ball to someone he would immediately demand the ball back. While other boys would play the ball, then wait to be brought back into the game, Paul would see his pass as the start of something he was going to be involved in. His passes were nearly always short one-twos; he rarely, if ever, went on a long run, merely hoping to get the ball. He oozed confidence and would go back and get the ball from the back-four defenders, so that he could start an attacking movement.

'Even at eleven, he showed what an emotional, quick-tempered and easily frustrated player he could be. If he was beaten by an opponent, he would get upset and angry; if the other lads did not do what he thought they should, he would get frustrated and moan; and if someone wasn't playing well, he would snap at them to make them try harder. He hated lack of effort. He ran his guts out for the team, and expected others to do the same.'

Paul had made up his mind, even then, it seems, to be a professional footballer. Most of the boys in that school team said they wanted to play for Newcastle United, but, according to Frank McGarry, Paul was the most insistent.

On the field he always had more drive and determination than other boys.

Off the field, however, he began to show less and less interest in lessons and he could not wait for school to finish, so he could be with his pals at Redheugh Boys' Club, where he was now playing regularly in five-a-side matches.

'He was a natural five-a-side player, always on the go, always making himself available,' says Tommy Leonard. 'Other kids seemed pre-occupied with their skills and tried to do too much. But Paul just played with the ball effortlessly. He'd always do something special in a game that made him stand out. He was a joy to watch.'

Five-a-sides and 'Doors' were all very well, and Paul revelled in them. But he longed to play in eleven-a-side games for the club, and kept pestering Tommy: 'When am I going to play in the big team, Mr Leonard?'

Tommy would smile, understandingly, and tell him to try to be patient; his time would come.

By normal standards, Paul's home life had never been settled. Not long after the family had moved to Dunston, a rather depressed, ill-kept part of Gateshead, a traumatic experience involving his father left the eleven-year-old boy distraught and more insecure than ever.

John Gascoigne had suffered severe migraine and black-outs ever since he fell badly and hit his head while playing football at the age of fifteen. Other members of his family had severe migraine, too, but none as bad as John; as he got older, the headaches got so bad he would have to sit in a quiet, darkened room. Nobody could pinpoint precisely what the trouble was or what could be done to ease the pain; John just had to live with it.

He did – for many years. And then, suddenly, the pain in his head exploded more violently and painfully than ever and John collapsed with a brain haemorrhage. It took a seven-hour operation at a Newcastle hospital to save him.

For John Gascoigne, the legacy of that terrible ordeal was a lifetime of unemployment. He had never been able to find regular work, but now he was warned he should not risk working again.

For his wife, Carol, it meant that a life that had never been easy would be harder than ever. With four children still at school, she had to become the breadwinner. She took jobs round the clock to pay the family bills; she made ropes; she worked at a Gateshead glass factory; she even valeted cars.

Paul, in his loneliness, turned to another family for comfort and consolation.

Over the past few months he had been seeing a lot of his St Cuthbert's soccer rival, Keith Spraggon. They were an unlikely mix: Keith was a quieter, more studious type, while Paul was boisterous and fun-loving. But they shared a common bond: they were both brilliant young footballers with potential to become professionals, and although their personalities were so different, they got on well. Keith's parents, Harry and Maureen Spraggon, liked the irrepressible kid with the impish grin and never-ending sense of fun, and encouraged his friendship with their son. Maureen, particularly, had a soft spot for Paul and would take him places and treat him to sweets.

When John Gascoigne's haemorrhage made Paul's home life even more difficult, Harry and Maureen willingly allowed the boy to sleep at their house, sometimes for days at a time. As Harry remembers today: 'Paul would come for the weekend and stay a fortnight. We didn't mind in the least. He was a good kid and he and Keith got on great.'

Keith remembers the days with affection. 'Paul was my best mate and we knocked about together all the time. I loved him coming to stay. He was a good laugh all the time and we were always mucking about.

'We never talked about his home life, but he used to look up to me, I think, because I had a little more than him.

'If he saw we had some ice cream in the fridge he'd ask if he could have some. One Saturday night, when my parents were out, I said he could have some ice cream if he dared to run across the field outside the house in his underpants and touch a tree.

'He agreed to do it immediately and stripped off. But after he'd touched the tree and was on his way back, I threw stones and muck at him, making him run off. Then I dashed inside and locked him out. I made him bang on the door for several minutes before letting him in. Then I gave him a whole block of ice cream and he scoffed the lot.

'It was a way of getting my own back, because Paul was always winding me up. But he could always take a joke himself.'

The Spraggons were an enormous support to Paul during one of the blackest, most worrying periods of his life. And that summer they shared the boys' excitement at the news that Redheugh's organizers were to launch an Under-13 team to compete in a new league the following season. Paul and Keith were only twelve, but they had been playing well enough against older boys, both at school and for Gateshead Boys, to stand a good chance of selection.

In spite of the problems at home in Malvern Close, Paul was a cheerful little boy when he broke up from Breckenbeds for the summer holidays.

And then, one July night, he walked round to Keith's house in Low Fell to go to the club. The tragedy that followed would leave Paul devastated and mentally scarred for ever.

3

On most evenings, Paul would walk from Malvern Close to Keith's home in Almond Crescent, and they would stroll to the boys' club together with another friend, Michael Kelly, who lived next door to Keith. Almond Crescent was some distance out of Paul's way, but he never seemed to mind, and he was normally early.

That summer of 1979, football training had not resumed, but on most nights the boys went to the club anyway, to play snooker or mini-badminton and generally mix with other friends. On the Thursday evening of 26 July, the three boys, in shorts and T-shirts, set off as usual, this time joined by Keith's nine-year-old brother, Steven.

At the time, there was a general stores on the corner of Derwentwater Road and Bensham Crescent, and the boys would always see it as fun to go in there and take the mickey out of a woman called Freda who served behind the counter.

At about 6.45 p.m. that evening, all four boys went into the shop and started their usual cheeky, sometimes abusive, banter.

Minutes later, Steven Spraggon dashed out of the shop, into Derwentwater Road in front of a parked ice-cream van, and was hit by an overtaking green Datsun. He was killed instantly.

Precisely why Steven ran into the road is not altogether clear.

The boys had been in the shop for some sweets and were standing outside laughing and carrying on when one of them shouted, 'Here comes Freda.' Steven ran straight across the pavement and on to Derwentwater Road in front of the ice-cream van.

Michael Kelly shouted, 'Watch out, there's a car coming,' and Keith tried to grab Steven, but just missed. When he was just a couple of steps out into the road, the car hit him.

Those are the facts.

What is a mystery, because Paul has never spoken publicly about the accident, is how he coped with the anguish and torment of seeing his best friend's brother killed in front of him – the most traumatic moments of his young life.

Certainly the tragedy devastated him and left him emotionally wrecked. But, according to Keith, he was affected physically, too. He started to have nightmares and wake up in the middle of the night, crying. Then he developed a stammer and a series of pronounced and bizarre nervous habits that became more noticeable the more anxious and tense he got.

Michael Kelly admits today that he himself still shudders at the terrible impact the accident had on him and everyone who knew Steven, both family and neighbours, and Redheugh Boys' Club, where he was an associate member.

'It all happened like a flash of lightning,' says Michael. 'One minute, Steven was there, with us – the next he was lying in the middle of the road, with blood coming out of his mouth as Keith cradled him in his arms.

'I ran off and phoned Keith's mam. I remember her running along Derwentwater Road in bare feet, holding her shoes, because she'd taken them off so she could run faster. I stood in the road with her and Keith, waiting for the ambulance to arrive.'

Michael went into such deep shock that he cannot remember what Paul did or where he went. But it seems that Michael's father drove Maureen Spraggon to the scene of the accident, then took Paul home to Malvern Close. Whether anyone was there to comfort him is not clear. 'The poor lad was crying and shaking like a leaf,' says Mr Kelly.

Before the funeral the following week, Paul and Michael and other young friends gathered in the Spraggon house. The coffin was in Steven's bedroom and Maureen asked the boys gently if they would mind going up and kissing him goodbye.

For Michael, it is the one moment from the whole terrible experience that he remembers most.

'We couldn't have refused to kiss Steven because it would have upset Mrs Spraggon,' he says. 'I went upstairs with her and he was lying there, all dressed up, and there

32

was the smell of lavender to keep the air fresh. Paul was there, of course, but I can't remember who he went upstairs with.

'The church was packed for the funeral and I couldn't stop crying when we sang the 23rd Psalm, *The Lord is My Shepherd*.

'Afterwards, I kept thinking about the accident all the time and would wake up in the middle of the night, frightened and panicking. I just couldn't understand or accept how it could have happened to Steven.'

The burly steelworker is not ashamed to admit that he still cries today when he sings the 23rd Psalm.

Paul and Keith were too upset to attend the first two sessions at Redheugh when training resumed. But they were encouraged to join the third and subsequent ones, for both the Spraggons and the club's organizers felt that being among their friends and playing football again would help the boys recover from the tragedy. Paul did admit to certain friends that the accident had really shaken him up, but would not speak about it. No one knew what to say to Keith, so nobody said anything and just tried to carry on as they had done before.

The Under-14 team coach, Terry Ritson, had to pick two teams to compete in the Northumberland Association of Boys' Clubs Under-14 League and a new league for the same age group, called the Gateshead Youth Consort. The season was due to kick off in September, but before that he had a chance to see how his lads performed in a five-a-side tournament at Newcastle's annual Tyneside Summer Exhibition and in two friendlies against other boys' club sides.

Paul was selected for the tournament and helped Redheugh battle through six rounds, involving more than 120 clubs, to the final. Sadly, they lost 2–1 to Montague Boys' Club, but Paul scored the goal, and the whole team were praised lavishly for doing so well in the tournament against boys all a year older. It was little consolation to the five Redheugh lads, however, and they all cried in disappointment.

Later that August, Terry Ritson had to select a team for the first friendly of the season, against Wallsend Boys' Club Under-12s. He always picked a squad of fourteen, but never named his final selection until just before the match, and excitement was high among the boys when they arrived at the club around nine o'clock that Sunday morning. For many, including Paul, it would be the first time they had played for the club in an eleven-a-side match on a grass pitch, and they all wanted to be in the team.

Ritson took all fourteen boys into the large kit room and told them to sit down. Then he told three of them that they would be substitutes for the match, watching their faces closely to make sure they took it well and were not too disappointed. Turning to the other eleven, he went through the team, one by one, telling each boy which position he would be playing. When he came to Paul, he said, 'I want you to play right midfield.'

A wide smile lit Paul's face. He was playing in the big team at last.

The match was played at the Shuttles, Redheugh's home ground in Eslington Park, and Paul, playing alongside his pal Keith, tore into the action from the first whistle. He was smaller and fatter than the Wallsend boys, and couldn't run as fast, but he had an aggressive will to win that gave him an edge and helped him win 50–50 tackles. His first touch with the ball was good and his distribution, both short, first-time balls, and long, crossfield passes, was deadly accurate.

Brian Clark, who ran Wallsend's Under-12s, had come to watch his own team, particularly Jeff Wrightson, Ian Bogie and Paul Stephenson. But he was quickly drawn to the little podgy boy controlling the midfield.

'Paul was the first boy to catch my eye that day,' Brian recalls. 'I noticed him almost immediately because he was so much smaller and fatter than the others, and had such natural skill and passing ability. I kept my eye on him, and as the game developed he shone out as the one who made things happen for his team.

'He was not frightened to use his weight to win the ball, and when he received a pass he controlled the ball with one touch, which enabled him to slip players as they tried to tackle him. He would run with the ball, but only ten yards or so, before laying it off. His passing was so accurate, the ball always went to the feet of a team-mate, or into a space for him. He had a good variation of passes and could hit a firm, short ball first time or find a player thirty yards away.

'I felt a bit sorry for him because, apart from Keith Spraggon, the players on his side were not as good. When he looked up with the ball, there were not too many players in position, wanting it. I thought it was a pity he was so tubby, because he was unable to get away from lighter, faster players. But I always looked for skill in a player and Paul certainly had that. He was very good.'

Understandably, Clark spent most of that game studying his own players. But he was a Newcastle United scout, and instinct told him he had witnessed something rather special that morning. As he left the Shuttles, delighted with Wallsend's 7–3 victory, Clark could not get the skilful, podgy little boy out of his mind, and he made a mental note of the funny name his team-mates had kept calling: 'Gazza . . . Gazza . . .'

What Brian Clark did not know was that the little terrier with the strange nickname had been spotted two years before by a rival scout. David Lloyd, a Middlesbrough scout living in Dunston, would go to Redheugh once a week to check on any new young talent. The Ayresome Park club had an arrangement with the organizers, who provided information on all new members, in return for an annual donation.

One evening, Lloyd had seen Paul and Keith playing. It was only a free-for-all kickabout in the playing yard, but both boys displayed such skill and artistry that Lloyd immediately saw the potential: their passes were so accurate, their control so confident, their vision so perceptive. Excited, Lloyd promised himself he would come back the following week to watch the boys again. They were just as brilliant, and Lloyd began to make notes about their progress in his scouting book.

The reports got longer and more detailed, and eventually Lloyd knew he would have to send them to the coaching chiefs at Ayresome Park: the two boys had more than mere potential – they had what it would take to make the grade.

Paul had impressed Terry Ritson, too. And when the squad assembled in that kit room again, on the second Sunday in September 1979, Ritson told him he was in the team for the first league match of the season against Kirkwood Boys' Club.

That afternoon, Paul crossed the Tyne Bridge and stepped proudly on to the pitch at the King George V Playing Fields in the Under-13s' new all-orange strip, with black trimmings. He had a quiet game in the team's 5–3 win, but he did not seem too disappointed. Why should he be? He'd played in his first league match in the 'big team' – and, in a couple of weeks, he was to have a trial for Gateshead Town's Under-13 side.

For a little boy knocked sideways with tragedy, it was a welcome, if brief, escape from the sadness burdening his young mind.

The aftermath of Steven's death began to affect Paul deeply, however. He had always enjoyed being treated, and spoiled, by Harry and Maureen, but now he would stay at their house more than ever – prompting Maureen to remark, 'Paul practically lives here.' He started being very protective towards her, insisting on escorting her to the bus stop on her way to work. He seemed to understand that Keith needed him, too, and gave himself generously to the relationship.

'Once,' Keith remembers, 'we went into Newcastle on

my birthday. Paul never had much money in his pocket, but on this day he bought me a record. Later, I saw another I wanted and went to buy it, but Paul insisted on buying that, too, even though it left him with nowt. He was a kind kid and generous to a fault. Everyone liked him.'

Paul was now less outgoing and boisterous, though: the tragedy had knocked the carefree banter out of him.

'He became very nervous – frightened, in a way,' says Keith. 'And when he used to sleep at our house, he'd lie awake at night, thinking about Steven and the accident. It really got to him.

'He began to stutter more and more, and then he'd blink all the time and start making funny noises. He couldn't help it; he was just plain nervous.'

At Breckenbeds, masters and pupils could not fail to notice the strange change.

George Stephenson, arts and crafts design teacher, says: 'The shock of that accident was so great, Paul developed a stammer, a twitch, and began blinking a lot. The tragedy hit him very hard. Steven Spraggon was killed right in front of him.

'Paul's afflictions were very noticeable, but it was played down. His parents arranged therapy, but he wasn't very secure.'

It says much for Harry and Maureen Spraggon that, in their own grief at losing such a dear little boy, they were willing, indeed able, to throw a comforting arm around Paul, and welcome him into their home so much and treat him like another son.

But, as that terrible year wore on and things slowly got back to normal, the caring couple began to sense the dangers of Paul staying at the house so much. Keith, they could see, was beginning to treat him more like a brother than a friend.

4

As the 1980–81 soccer season started, it was Keith, not
Paul, whom most people considered the better, stronger,
all-round player. And when Newcastle's youth development
officer, Brian Watson, heard that Middlesbrough had taken
a close interest in Keith, he told the two scouts under his
command, Brian Clark and Peter Kirkley, to check him
out as well.

One evening in the second week of September, Kirkley
went to the now-demolished Beacon Rise School to watch
Keith in one of two 25-minute trial games for that season's
Gateshead Boys' Under-14 team.

It took Kirkley only a few minutes to decide that, despite
all the good reports, Keith was not a boy he felt would
make it as a pro.

There was another boy due to play in the second trial,
who did not look the part either. Peter had watched him
knocking about on his own on the sidelines during the first
game and was intrigued. The boy was astonishingly clever
with the ball, but looked all wrong: while other boys were
athletically well-defined and looked strong, this one was
podgy, with puppy fat on his face and legs, and he was so
small he did not look as though he could last the pace on a
big football pitch. As a juggler he was good, but Peter
knew that jugglers, however brilliant, do not always make
good players. He wondered why the little boy was there.

The second trial started. And as soon as the ball was
played to the little fat boy in the middle of the field,
Kirkley knew why he was there.

For he produced an instinctive flash of skill that made
Kirkley blink in disbelief: the boy brought the ball down
with his right foot, and instead of moving off to his left,

knocked the ball against his left foot and swayed off swiftly to his right, past a challenging opponent – all, it seemed, in the same split-second movement. It was a breathtakingly precocious piece of artistry from someone so young, and Peter Kirkley wondered if he was seeing things; feeling a rush of excitement, he decided to watch the boy closely to make sure it wasn't just luck.

Keith Spraggon now forgotten, Peter watched the little boy intently for the rest of the match. When it was over, he walked up to John Brabban, a schoolteacher in charge of the trials, and asked him who the boy was and if he could have him on trial at Newcastle United.

On that Gateshead playing field that mild September evening, Paul Gascoigne's destiny in the game he was born to play had been mapped out.

One is tempted to wonder, however, if Newcastle would have heard of him if Kirkley had not gone there to watch Keith Spraggon. And, indeed, if Paul had not produced that fleeting flash of ingenuity early in that match. For Kirkley admits that Paul did not have a good game; he's not sure if he even made the next trial.

'Paul wasn't in the game much at all,' says Kirkley. 'If his teachers were looking for someone to win a match for them, it certainly wasn't him. He just wasn't fit enough to go on surging runs and score goals or create chances.

'But I saw enough that evening to convince me he had something you can't put there. Football clubs have experienced people who can bring out talent, but they can't put it in; they can't make a racehorse out of a donkey.

'All the flair players are born with this "something" and Paul was one of them. In that trial, another ball was played into him and he chested it down expertly. It's not an easy piece of skill and most young schoolboys wouldn't have had the courage to try it. But Paul did it comfortably.'

Kirkley's mentor was Joe Harvey, the former Newcastle captain, who became assistant manager and chief scout before he died in 1989. Harvey had a saying when he was reporting on possible trialists. If he liked a boy, he'd say, 'He has a trick.' If he didn't, he'd say, 'He hasn't got a trick.' Kirkley picked up the saying from him.

And although he did not see Paul as a 'finished product', he went into the club's St James's Park ground the morning after the trial and reported to Brian Watson. 'There's this kid, Paul Gascoigne. He's got a trick.'

One Sunday morning, two months later, Brian Clark went to watch Keith in a Redheugh home game. He liked what he saw: Keith was bigger and stronger than most of the opposition and ran around a lot, winning the ball. But, again, the player who caught Brian's eye was the one he remembered being impressed with in that August friendly the previous year – the one they called 'Gazza'. He turned to one of the parents, watching from the touchline. 'Who *is* that fat little lad?'

'Paul Gascoigne,' the parent replied.

That night, Clark had a drink with Brian Watson in the Rising Sun in Wallsend.

'So what do you think of young Spraggon?' Watson asked.

'He's a very good player,' Clark said. 'But a kid called Paul Gascoigne is better.'

'Don't be stupid,' Watson scoffed. 'You're kidding me.'

Clark recalls today: 'Spraggon was the one everyone was talking about – and that's who Brian wanted to hear about. I kept telling him Gascoigne was the better player, but he wouldn't have it. He was disappointed in me and we changed the subject.'

After that 1980 Christmas, a Wallsend match was called off because of bad weather and Clark went to the Shuttles to watch a Redheugh game. Paul had a blinder, outplaying everyone and generally running the show.

That evening, he met Watson in a working men's club and raved about Paul's performance. But, again, his Newcastle boss did not want to know. 'You're barmy, you are,' he said.

But Clark would not let the matter drop and they had a row, which ended with Watson fuming, 'Right – you're sacked – you're finished.'

'He was only half joking, but I bit on it and lost my temper,' Clark remembers. 'It was a bad night.'

The following Tuesday, David Lloyd, the Middlesbrough scout in Gateshead, and one of Clark's colleagues at a Newcastle engineering firm, came up to him and said, 'I hear you've been chasing my lads.'

Clark was taken aback by the confrontation. But he was stunned when Lloyd told him that Keith and Paul had been going to Ayresome Park for Sunday training for over a year.

'What's more,' said Lloyd 'both of them are going to sign schoolboy forms for Middlesbrough.'

Clark went straight to a phone and called Brian Watson at St James's Park. 'You think I'm barmy, do you, Watty?' he said. 'Well, Middlesbrough don't think I'm stupid – Gascoigne's going to sign for them.'

After Lloyd's early progress reports, Middlesbrough had been further impressed with Paul at a series of FA coaching courses at Gateshead Stadium, run in conjunction with Gateshead Education Authority, which placed enormous emphasis on nurturing local schoolboy talent.

Only that summer, Paul had been back to Dukeshousewood for another weekend of coaching. He and dozens of skilful Gateshead boys stayed in army-style barracks for three days, and had nothing else to think about but football. There were five-a-side and eleven-a-side games, penalty competitions – and they were coached by famous professionals from all over the country.

Ian Hornby, who now works as a coach with former England Under-21 manager Dave Sexton in Saudi Arabia, spent six years organizing those coaching clinics, and remembers Paul not so much as a football prodigy but as a clown.

'Some of the boys were better footballers than Paul, but

as a joker he was in a class of his own,' says Hornby. 'One afternoon it poured down and we had to keep the lads occupied inside a shelter hut for two and a half hours. The boys were playing cards and listening to records and having ball-trick contests. But they all got a bit bored and things went quiet for a bit until Paul stood up on a three-foot high stage at one end of the room and started telling jokes.

'He was brilliant and not at all nervous. He told about three or four jokes, grinning cheekily all the time, and had everyone falling about laughing.

'Other lads followed him, then Paul got back up another couple of times. The lads were cheering and clapping him. He was the star of the show and loved the attention.

'He was very popular on those trips and all the lads warmed to him. He went round in a crowd of four or five and seemed to be the leader. The other boys looked up to him and he was the one doing most of the talking. He loved those weekends and came back year after year.'

Paul's second year at Breckenbeds proved to be no more distinguished than his first; academic study still took second place to football, and when he wasn't thinking about what future Middlesbrough might hold for him, Paul was thinking about the boys' club. He was never happier than when each school day ended and he could get to Redheugh for some serious playing.

'He seemed to spend his life there,' says Paul Donnelly, who played with Paul for Gateshead Boys' and Redheugh. 'He was good at everything – particularly playing the fool. And he was a bit of a loudmouth who always had something to say.

'I remember him as a lad who wasn't too well off. His trousers had holes in them and his sand shoes were a bit knocked about. And he seemed to be always in the same jumper and T-shirt.

'Some lads were spoiled and had the best of everything. But Paul would struggle. When his football boots were ripped, he would not automatically get another pair. He'd say, "My boots are knackered", and have to scrape round to borrow a pair. I lent him my spare pair once or twice. Other lads lent him theirs, too.

'I first met Paul when we were ten. I was taking the mickey out of his name and he said he was going to chin me. But it was only a jokey thing, and we became friends.'

To many people who didn't know him, Paul Gascoigne was an arrogant boy with too much to say for himself and a cocky way of saying it. But his self-assertiveness came from being born in a poor area where he had to fight for what little he got, and he was totally without malice or vindictiveness. He was a likeable and popular lad, who was welcomed in the homes of his friends.

Michael Kelly, who also played with Paul as a child, said: 'As an area, Dunston was as low down the scale as you could go, and we couldn't fail to notice how differently Paul was living. He would go to other people's homes and sort of cling on. He seemed to go from one family to the next.

'He didn't get a lot because his parents didn't have much money. He used to come to our house and my mam would always give him some of our dinner. He'd often eat at Keith's house, too. It wasn't because Paul was a scrounger or anything like that – it was just because his father and mother weren't there for him a lot of the time, that's all.

'It was always football this or football that with Paul. Five of us used to play a knockout game called Cups: one was goalkeeper and the other four trying to score. When a player scored, he would sit down behind the goal. The one who didn't score was knocked out and the three left would start again until there was only two left for the final – usually Paul and Keith.

'Paul would always pretend he was the best professional player of the moment. He'd say, "I'll be Kevin Keegan", or whoever he'd seen score the best goal on Match of the Day, and Keith would be someone else. In those games, Keith nearly always won – no one could get the ball off him.'

As that 1980–81 season wore on, Paul had developed his skills so much that boys who had been playing with him at school and in the Redheugh and town sides began to notice a marked change in him.

'It was noticeable that he was getting better and better while the rest of us stayed the same,' says Paul Morris, who had played with Paul at eleven. 'We were all still good, but he was outstanding and went round players with even more ease, even though he was still smaller than everyone else.

'There was always something about Paul that made him different from other boys. And as he got older and better, you felt he would go on to be something special.'

Just before Christmas, a third professional club – Ipswich – began showing an interest in Gateshead's dynamic footballing duo. The East Anglian side's North East scout, John Carruthers, had seen Paul and Keith play for Redheugh and, like other people, had been impressed, particularly by the tubby little boy with the magic feet.

Carruthers went to watch the boys again, at a Gateshead Boys' match, and clashed with David Lloyd.

Lloyd lived near Malvern Close and had arranged to drive Paul home after the game. As Paul came out of the changing room, Carruthers offered him a lift, too. Lloyd stepped in. And for a few seconds, the scouts each held Paul's arms as they argued about who was taking him. Finally, Paul stuck to the original arrangement and went home with Lloyd.

In February, Carruthers saw Paul play another blinder and knew he had to let the then Ipswich manager, Bobby Robson, have a look. Having got permission from Paul's headmaster to approach the boy's parents, Carruthers went to their home in Dunston.

He recalls: 'Paul answered the door and I told him I was the scout from Ipswich Town and showed him my card. His face lit up and I could sense the excitement going through his mind. He said his dad wasn't there and his

44

mum was working. I told him I thought he was a good footballer and wanted to take him down to Ipswich. Would he like to go?

'Paul gave a huge smile and said, "Oh, yes, I'd love to." He told me his mum was working at a garage and gave me directions. As I said goodbye, I shook his hand. I'll always remember walking away and looking back and seeing him at the door, smiling. His handshake wasn't as big as that smile.

'The garage was nearby and I found Mrs Gascoigne hoovering cars. I told her Paul was delighted that I wanted to take him to Ipswich and she said, "He would be – he's football daft. I'd be delighted for him to go down with you." It was obvious how thrilled she was for him.'

Paul was equally thrilled that Carruthers wanted Keith to go too. And one Sunday, early in April, both boys and fourteen others from different parts of Scotland and the North East travelled to Ipswich by minibus for their trials.

During the journey, Carruthers – chairman of the North East Scouts Association – put on a Strauss waltz cassette and saw Paul in a mirror, grinning and nudging one of his mates, as if to say, 'Hey look at that old fogey.'

'I changed the tape and put on some loud pop music,' Carruthers remembers. 'Then I told them: "If you listen to this stuff, you'll be so deaf you won't hear when your mates shout for the ball on the field – so listen to Strauss instead!"'

During the five-day stay, a Tyne-Tees TV documentary crew were filming a programme called *Robson's Choice*, which showed Bobby choosing young schoolboys to sign. Although the film concentrates on an older group of youngsters, Paul and the other lads are seen on the programme. At one point Paul, standing next to Keith, is listening to John Wark, one of Ipswich's first-team players, cracking a joke; the camera pans to Paul who gives a big smile. Later, he is glimpsed getting Robson's autograph in the club's car park.

The whole experience, it seems, was overwhelming for a lad who had not travelled much in his thirteen years. Don Campbell, a coach who helped Carruthers on that trip, remembers Paul being very quiet when the boys were taken on a tour of the club before they left. 'The lad was over-awed,' he says. 'He walked round with his eyes wide open, taking it all in, but too overwhelmed to say much.

'He loved getting autographs and was always the first to get a signature when the first-teamers finished training. I remember him gazing up at Terry Butcher, Mick Mills, Paul Mariner and the others in adulation, and probably a bit of envy, too. I honestly don't think he could take in that he was really there.'

Paul and the other lads who travelled to Ipswich were rejected. And, on the evidence of the trial, Bobby Robson made the right decision with Paul.

'He was a little boy lost that week,' says Carruthers. 'He was playing with some very good boys who were a lot stronger than him. He lacked pace and couldn't get the ball enough to show his skill, which was what he needed to do to catch Bobby's eye.

'Paul knew he hadn't done himself justice. He came off after one game, scowling and a bit upset, because he'd hardly touched the ball. But it wasn't long before he was smiling again.

'I think I took Paul too early. If I'd waited a year for him to mature, it may have been different. At the end of the trials, when Bobby had given the lads the bad news, I advised Paul to get in the school gym and do some training, lose some weight – he could come back next year when he had gained a yard or two. Instead of being gloomy he took it well and said something along the lines of, "Aye, I will, sir." He was such a happy little fellow – always laughing and joking.'

What probably helped Paul to be not too despondent was Robson's upbeat manner when he told the boys they hadn't made it. Ipswich's decision was not the end of their footballing dreams, he said: he himself had not got into football until 17½ – and he was playing for England at the age of twenty-three.

Neither Paul nor Keith had time to dwell on whatever disappointment they may have felt: they had to leave Ipswich promptly and get back to Newcastle in time to play for Redheugh in a cup final.

Terry Ritson picked them up at the station and drove them to the ground. Then he suggested the team went out to look at the pitch and have a quiet team talk.

'Most of the lads were keyed up and a bit tense,' Ritson recalls. 'When I took them back to the dressing room an argument broke out with all the lads complaining they had the wrong boots. I noticed Paul in a corner laughing his head off. Somehow he had got back into the dressing room without anyone seeing and swapped all the boots around for a laugh. He was always doing that sort of thing.

'His little joke certainly worked that night. It broke the tension and the lads went out and played really well to win 5–0. Paul got a hat-trick.'

With Ipswich out of the running, it now seemed likely that Paul would sign for Middlesbrough. But then, that Easter, Peter Kirkley – with, perhaps, some help from Brian Clark – persuaded Newcastle's chief scout, Brian Watson, to travel to Ayr, in Scotland, where Paul was playing for Redheugh in an international boys' club tournament.

It was the turning point – the weekend that truly shaped Paul's football future. For he had a brilliant tournament, and Brian Watson was as impressed as anybody. At last he had seen for himself – seen what Clark and Kirkley had seen. And he knew he had to have the lad at St James's Park.

Says Clark: 'I met Brian in the Jubilee Club when he came back, and he was full of Paul. He thought the lad was very good and could be something special. He didn't say "Well done" to me; he never even acknowledged that I'd raved about Paul many months before. But it didn't matter. I was just delighted that, at last, he'd seen Paul and agreed with me – and that the boy was going to get a chance in the game.'

Paul's birthday, 27 May, was only days away – and it was crucial to Watson because clubs were forbidden to sign boys before their fourteenth birthday. Watson, convinced Paul wanted to sign for Middlesbrough, had to move quickly if he was to persuade him to go to St James's Park. He decided to woo Paul's parents. And he said enough to convince them that their son should sign with him, because on Sunday evening – the day before his birthday – Paul knocked on David Lloyd's door nearby in Dunston. He was crying.

'I'm sorry, Mr Lloyd,' he sobbed. 'I'm going to sign for Newcastle.'

5

For Paul and Keith, it was the beginning of the end of a deep friendship.

Paul had been staying at Keith's house more and more following Steven's death and it started bothering Harry and Maureen Spraggon. As gently as they could, they told Keith he should try to see less of his best friend.

'They began to worry about Paul always being here,' says Keith today. 'They said he could never take Steven's place. They felt we should drift apart and have our own lives. I think my mam had a word with Paul's mam, because he did stop coming to our house so much.

'They were right, I think; Paul seemed to be there all the time, just as Steven had been. I enjoyed Paul's company and it helped me come to terms with our loss, but I do think I began to look on him as a brother.

'I was very disappointed that he went to Newcastle, because we'd always talked about playing together at Middlesbrough. We used to like being in the same team and playing the ball to each other. I think Paul wanted to be with me at Middlesbrough, but his father told me he would never have his son play there. I remember Paul telling David Lloyd, and crying, that he wanted to sign but couldn't. I never got around to asking him why.'

The two friends began to see less of each other and drifted further and further apart. Keith had signed for Middlesbrough and it seemed likely the two boys would meet up again on the soccer pitch, as professionals on opposing sides – friendly rivals again, as they had been at school.

But fate would send one boy on to football glory and the other, arguably the more gifted, into relative obscurity, working for a cash-and-carry store.

For Keith Spraggon, it seems, the pain of losing a brother that tragic July night took away something deep down that he never got back. Talented though he was, the dedication needed to make it professionally was simply not there.

For Paul, the tears dried quickly, and he could not wait to tell his pals at Redheugh that he had been signed as a schoolboy for Newcastle.

'He was dead proud,' Paul Donnelly recalls. 'I was playing snooker when he came in, showing an official-looking green card he had been given, proving he was a Newcastle United schoolboy.'

Training for the schoolboys was held at United's ground at Benwell every Tuesday evening from 6.30 until 8.30, and Paul would have to get two buses – one from Gateshead into Newcastle, then another to Benwell. In the summer the boys trained outside, but from October until February they stayed in the gym. In the holidays they trained from 10 a.m. until 12 and then, after lunch, did an afternoon session until 4 p.m.

Jimmy Nelson, a former professional footballer and schoolteacher, who was Newcastle's junior team coach, remembers Paul as just one of a good bunch.

He says: 'I got the impression Paul was aware he was now alongside really good players and would have to prove himself if he was to get on. He was a bit intimidated in the early days, but as he got to know everyone better, and became more confident in training, he was the life and soul of the party.

'If we organized a trip away, he'd always be the one standing up in the coach cracking jokes and making everyone laugh. He was good fun and always had a smile on his face – a joy to have around.

'In training matches, Paul's close ball control was the outstanding feature of his game and he was excellent at one- or two-touch. The only thing that let him down was his stamina: his physique didn't seem made for running. He had all the skills necessary, but I did have my doubts and felt that, if anything was going to stop him making it, it would be his stamina and physical strength.'

There was nothing wrong with Paul's stamina, however, if there was a ball around. Once the morning session had ended, he would still be out there kicking about for another twenty minutes or so. He would practise hitting the ball into one of the stanchions – between the crossbar and a post – so that it got stuck there. One of the other lads would go in goal and Paul would test himself from all different angles around the penalty area, always aiming for the same spot.

In the race to sign Paul, the reserve team manager, Willie McFaul, had gone to Breckenbeds School to get the necessary approval from the headmaster and find out something about Paul. Nobody faulted his football ability, but the head and a couple of teachers did make it plain that the boy's attitude to work was questionable at times.

Certainly that summer his attitude to work as a proud Newcastle schoolboy was faultless. And it would continue to impress Jimmy Nelson over the next couple of years while he was at his new school.

The following September, Paul began his two-year spell at the 'big' school, Heathfield High, in Low Fell. He could hardly have got off to a worse start. After meeting Clive Hepworth, who was to be his form master, he went into his first lesson – and lasted just twenty minutes.

The lesson was art, and the teacher, one Jean Hedley, was a strict, no-nonsense lady who had a rather old-fashioned approach to teaching. She knew nothing about the thirty or so boys and girls who sat down in her class that September morning; but one thing they would know soon enough is that she would not tolerate lack of attention during a lesson, particularly among children on their first day at a new school.

Paul, it appears, was not in the mood for art: he could not draw particularly well and probably felt that, for him, the lesson was a waste of time. So he chose the moment to get to know his new friends; to let them know he was a bit of a livewire, with something to say for himself. His attitude did not go down well with Mrs Hedley.

'He was as mad as a hatter,' she says today. 'He was bouncing up and down and generally paying no attention whatever. I had to warn him almost immediately that if he didn't calm down, I would send him out.'

Paul's lack of interest in Mrs Hedley's endeavours was not helped when she gave them their first task. If she had asked them to draw a football or a goal, even a player in Newcastle United kit, she may have got a better response from Paul. As it was, she asked him and the rest of the class to draw a flower. And it left him even more un-interested than ever.

'I think flowers are wonderful, but I'm sure Paul thought, what a load of rubbish having to draw one,' she says. 'He didn't even try to make a good effort. He just drew a straight line for the stem, a ragged circle for the flower head, and a few crooked triangles for the petals. He did it very quickly, then started talking out of turn and generally distracting other children again. I have never stood for that kind of misbehaviour, so I told him he was to leave the class. I told him to go to another teacher – and that was the last I saw of Paul Gascoigne.'

Sadly, it was to be a familiar story in many other subjects: Paul showed little interest in anything except sport, and several teachers complained about his behaviour to Clive Hepworth.

Most of their complaints were justified, but one, involving his nervous habits, was not.

Tennis coach Jeff Lambert says: 'As well as a stammer, Paul developed a nervous swallow – a clearing of the throat, which came out as a high-pitched squeak. He wouldn't be able to control it and some teachers would order him out of their classes because they thought he was taking the mickey – or trying to attract attention to himself by being stupid.

'But some muscular reaction forced the noise out, particularly when he was under pressure, and there was nothing Paul could do about it. This nervous habit didn't do him any favours in lessons. But some other things *did* get him into trouble.'

'He *was* an irritant to an extent,' Mr Hepworth concedes. 'If there was a job to be done, he really didn't want to know about it. He'd do it as quickly as possible to get it out of the way and say, "That's good enough." A teacher trying to encourage children to pass an exam wants them to try a bit more.

'I quickly realized that Paul was never going to be academical. He gave the impression he thought academic work was a bit of a nuisance and he'd far rather spend his time playing sport.'

Paul was in class 4D, which was the lower end of Heathfield's academic scale. Although not regarded by staff as D-for-Dunce, the class was the third of three classes which would concentrate on a relatively easy art bias, not tough science subjects such as chemistry and physics.

Paul's modest success was limited to English language and environmental studies; he struggled with anything that involved a lot of reading, such as geography and history.

'No great intelligence is needed for those subjects, but you have to sit down and learn the stuff,' says Mr Hepworth. 'Paul, like many others in that form, didn't see the point in doing that, couldn't see how it could help him.

'He had no enthusiasm or positive approach to many other subjects; he would just go through the motions. When there is no interest, children get bored and chat, and generally disrupt the class. This happened with Paul, and certain teachers he didn't get on with would come to me, complaining about him.

'When I spoke to him, Paul would just say he was not any good at whatever subject we were discussing. I'd urge him to play the game and behave for a while and the trouble would pass.

'I didn't get heavy with him; as his form master, I couldn't afford to alienate him, or things would have got worse. I just pulled the reins in. Paul was never involved in anything serious, such as bullying or violent behaviour; he was a cheeky chap who liked a bit of fun and sometimes overstepped the mark. So I made it clear to him that a joke was all right, but he had to learn how far he could go; to know when the joke was over and when he had to work.

'Sometimes when I made him really get down to it, he didn't get on with *me*. He just didn't see the point in learning.

'I quickly discovered that he would respond to anything to do with football – the kid was absolutely soccer-mad. I am a keen Middlesbrough fan and he was devoted to Newcastle, so we would have the occasional banter and difference of opinion.

'He would tease me that Boro were the weakest of the big three North-East sides, that we had poor support and hadn't won a significant trophy. He would poke fun at our supporters for not being as fanatical as Newcastle's, and generally take the rise out of my team.

'At break-time, we would chat about football and what games had been on TV. And on Mondays I would take the mickey out of Newcastle if they had lost and Middlesbrough had won. Paul would take it good-naturedly and bounce back. He always had a cheeky grin on his face and would react quickly with humour and a quip, never aggression. He was a real cheeky charlie who made the other children laugh. He was very popular.

'In geography, I got Paul and some of the others to appreciate the location of industrial towns in the North East by running through the football teams while looking at a map. It was one of the few areas he clicked into. He could relate to something he would otherwise have found tedious.'

Other teachers were not so willing to woo Paul's interest with a football angle, however, and his lack of enthusiasm for anything remotely academic continued throughout that first year. His lack of interest bred boredom and misbehaviour, and he had to be disciplined, says Mr Hepworth, 'for the odd daft thing'. But, generally, Paul felt so vulnerable, threatened and unconfident in class that he kept his head down and seemed to treat school as a necessary evil he had to tolerate.

Certainly his attendance record was good; and, despite having a three-mile trek from Dunston every morning, he was nearly always at school at least half an hour before the 8.55 a.m. start. Like other pupils, he wore the school uniform: black blazer, black trousers and white shirt, dark blue tie with light blue stripes, and grey jumper. He had hard-soled shoes, but wore black trainers whenever he could and, in more rebellious days, he swapped his school uniform for a pair of baggy, purple-lined, grey trousers which were covered in zips and had pockets almost down to the knees. Paul loved wearing those trousers and teachers finally gave up nagging him not to wear them.

Paul's love of sport, and football in particular, helped keep him involved in the school when, otherwise, he might have rebelled.

'I don't think he thought it was worth the effort to kick against the system,' says Mr Hepworth. 'He just got on with school life. Sport kept his interest and he didn't get into any serious trouble, such as crime, as some kids do. His excesses were restricted to banter and humour, and he remained, happily contained, in the school community.'

Paul's attitude to work filtered through to John Brabban, who took PE, and whenever Peter Kirkley rang up for a progress report the teacher found it easy. 'I had to be blunt and tell him that Paul wasn't going great guns academically because he was too busy wanting to play football for Newcastle United,' says Mr Brabban. Peter appreciated Paul's keenness, but was a little worried; pro clubs do like to see a boy do well in lessons as well as on the field.

The confidence Paul lacked in the classroom came out on the pitch, of course. And although Heathfield's fourth-year team was weaker than previous years, it never stopped Paul playing his heart out.

'He was a terrier and tried to do everything for the side,' says John Brabban. 'He'd even take throw-ins. He had a good, long throw on him, but he would go for the short throw, so that he could get the ball back. He was all over the pitch, taking corners, free kicks – in attack or defence – penalties, and goal kicks. He was only small, but his timing was so good he took floating goal kicks – far better than the bigger lads. If the keeper had a go and messed it up, Paul would say, "I'll take the next one, eh?" He loved dominating a game and being involved all the time. If the ball went out of play, Paul would dash after it, while others walked around, glad of a rest. Paul just wanted to get on with the game.

'It was not a good team and Paul would try his best to encourage the other lads. He was a tough tackler and thought nothing of getting stuck in to the biggest opponent, even though he was so small. He'd get his less brave team-mates to get stuck in, too. He'd gee them up, then a moment later put in a tough challenge to show them how it was done. He would never moan at, or criticize, his team-mates, though. And I never saw him answering back a referee.

'Paul was so committed to the game. Once, he turned up for a game with 'flu. It wasn't just a slight cold – he was really sick. But he still insisted on playing and ran his heart out that game. Paul virtually crawled off the pitch, having given everything, and he was so ill he was off school the next day.

'In the changing rooms boys were always comparing their gear. When anyone asked Paul what sort of boots he had, he'd say, "They're my Woolworth's specials!" He was never able to afford an expensive pair of boots, but it never seemed to bother him. I remember it always gave the other lads a good laugh when he called his boots that.'

If you can really play football, if you have that genuine touch of class, it does not matter what you have on your feet. And, in certain situations, it does not matter who you have on your side, either. In lunchtime five-a-side matches in the gym, for instance, Paul was so much better than everyone else that he would deliberately choose to play with the four worst players to give himself a challenge. He seemed anxious to prove to people that he was a good player, no matter who was on his side, and that he did not need good players around him to make him look good.

Jeff Lambert said, 'Paul would think, "I'm the only good player, so, if we win, it's because of me." He was playing for himself, of course, but he would encourage his less-able team-mates and help them to improve their game.

'He had an amazing ability to dance round people in the gym. And if some of the better players on the other side got cocky, Paul would dribble round them as if to show them who was best. He'd push it through their legs, go on to score, then run round the gym as if on a lap of honour, waving a finger in the air – something he'd always done when he scored a goal.'

Even then, in 1981, the Heathfield teachers who marvelled at Paul's rare skill wondered if his erratic temperament would outweigh his playing ability when it came to a career in the game.

John Brabban summed Paul up: 'We all felt that his lack of discipline on the field was the only thing that could jeopardize his professional footballing future. He enjoyed entertaining and was always a character to express himself in a very artistic way. But it was always: win at all costs.'

Normally, sport was too important to Paul to misbehave and risk being banned from taking part. But, on one occasion, he did get up to a typical bit of mischief that left him with a sore backside.

Alan Cooke, who took games, had an extra large group in the gym one day, so when the boys went into the changing room, he told them to hang their clothes on the shower heads.

Immediately after the lesson, Mr Cooke went into the changing room and caught Paul standing on a chair in the shower area with his hand on a tap, clearly about to turn it on to drench other lads' clothes.

'What *are* you doing, Gascoigne?' Mr Cooke demanded to know, angrily.

'It wasn't me, sir,' Paul replied, unblinkingly.

'Come here,' said Mr Cooke, no doubt angrier still at being taken for a fool.

Today, Mr Cooke says: 'I got him into the changing room and told him to bend over. Then I took off my training shoe and walloped him once on the bottom. All the other lads had now come into the changing room and were watching, delighted that someone else, not them, was on the receiving end of my wallops.

'I didn't do it as a major punishment – just a reminder to all the boys that I was the gaffer. Paul didn't resent it.

He thought it was a fair cop and afterwards just rubbed his backside and walked off to get changed. Knowing Paul, he was probably grinning to his pals.

'All the boys fall into certain categories and Paul is what I call a smiler. When I knew him, he was happy with his lot and always grinning. He liked to muck around and have a practical joke, but when he did overstep the mark he accepted getting collared. He was not the type to stay out of mischief for too long and I must have disciplined him lots of times, although I can't remember specifically when.'

Form master Clive Hepworth did not have that problem, however; in those first three months, Paul had made a marked impression on him, not always, perhaps, for the right reasons. And he remembers a specific incident when Paul was lucky to get away with just a telling-off.

It was the last day of term and Hepworth had to go to the off-licence to buy drinks for the staff Christmas party. He had left it to the last minute and did not want to be delayed.

As he was setting off for the shop, a boy came flying down the stairs and tumbled in front of him. As he lay on the floor, the boy looked up at Hepworth, then at another boy at the top of the stairs. 'He pushed me, sir, it's his fault,' he shouted.

The last thing Hepworth wanted was a problem, but he knew he had to deal with the incident. He helped the boy to his feet then glared at the other one on the stairs. But before he could say anything Paul grinned and said, 'It wasn't me, sir.'

For the first time since joining Redheugh as that impish eight-year-old, Paul was unhappy with his football.

After breaking into the Under-13 side at the age of twelve, he had been a star player and one of the first on the team sheet for whatever side he played. But, in 1981, the club did not have an Under-15 team and Paul, now fourteen, found himself in a frustrating position: he was too old for the Under-14s and too small for the Under-16s. Keith Spraggon made the side because he had developed that much more and could hold his own with the older boys. But Paul was still tubby and relatively slow, and while no one questioned his skill and ability, he was not considered strong enough for that league. He was selected for the squad but, more often than not, watched the matches from the touchline.

Paul wanted to be a player, not a spectator, and when his father told him he could get him a game for a rival club, Dunston Juniors, Paul jumped at the chance. What his father did not tell him was that Redheugh's permission should have been requested under the 'seven-day rule', which had been introduced to stop players being 'poached'. If Paul's father had written to Redheugh, saying that his son wanted to play for Dunston, permission could have been given and the 'transfer' made official. As it was, Dunston Juniors did not bother to write to Redheugh until after Paul had turned out for them.

John Gascoigne's underhand behaviour rankled with Tommy Leonard and his colleagues, particularly since they had made an exception for the under-age Paul to join the club all those years before.

Evan Bryson says today: 'Paul's dad didn't have the courtesy to tell us he was taking Paul to another club. We would not have caused any problems over that, but we did not appreciate him not going through the correct procedure.

'We could have ordered an inquiry, but we didn't want to drag Paul into anything. After all, it was not really down to him how things were done. He just wanted to play football.

'He had become a bit miserable that season. He was the type of lad who wasn't happy if you took the ball away from his feet. We wanted to play him, but it was too rough. He was tubby and small and would only have got kicked around.

'He was in the squad for an away match against Montague Boys' Club, but when I arrived I discovered he was not even a substitute. The coach told me, "It's not his sort of game. Those lads are too heavy. He doesn't stand a chance – he'll just get roughed up."

'I looked at Paul. He was so unhappy. It wasn't often he didn't have a smile on his face, but that day he was really miserable and just wandered around the outside of the pitch on his own, kicking one of the spare balls.

'I think he sensed it was the beginning of the end for him at Redheugh. He knew that if he couldn't play football with us, he had to move on. It was sad for us, because he was such an enjoyable boy to have around, and, probably, we weren't fully aware of his problems.'

It more than saddened Tommy Leonard. At Redheugh, the organizers had always taken a pride in running a proper club, with a strict code of behaviour, and Paul had never been in the least undisciplined. Dunston Juniors, however, was run from a pub and discipline was not a top priority. Paul was even sent off for dirty play – something that had never happened at Redheugh. 'Dunston nearly ruined Paul,' says Tommy.

The 'transfer' was completed in the proper manner and Paul stopped going to the club that had been his life, and didn't even say goodbye to the people who had been his friends for more than five years.

A naturally gifted sports player, Paul shone at all PE, particularly basketball and tennis. And when he joined Jeff Lambert's tennis lessons in the summer term of his first year, he showed such good technique and fighting spirit that he was immediately classed as a candidate for the school's five-boy team.

'He didn't have any equipment that first day, so he went to the sports store room and picked out a cheap old blue wooden racket, which he then claimed as his.

'Paul had never played, but he had a natural action and a

very strong forehand, which, at schoolboy level, is usually good enough to win games. Paul caught the tennis bug and you couldn't keep him off the court. He had an aggressive sporting attitude and always wanted to be the winner – even in lessons.

'He preferred to play singles because then he could be really competitive. He would go 2–5 down, but was such a fighter he would come back and win. He seemed to know he could get back on top.

'His psychological approach always gave him the edge. He'd run and fight for everything – never let anything go. There was never any point in putting him in a game that was just a friendly – he just couldn't play that way. If his opponent was weaker, Paul would still serve as hard. As far as he was concerned, he was there to win.

'He was never afraid to try to psych out his opponent. If Paul was winning, he would go to the net and ask the score, just to remind his rival who was on top. And let everyone watching know, too.

'At schoolboy level they kept their own scores, and when they changed ends Paul would say innocently, "That's 5–2 to me, isn't it?" when he clearly knew the score. It was a psychological ploy that often made his opponents lose concentration.

'Paul's confidence gave him a big advantage. He wouldn't be frightened to tell his opponent he was a better player and that he was going to win.

'He was always a nervous boy to talk to and he had a slight stutter. But that would disappear on the court and he'd become a cocky little lad, oozing self-confidence. If he thought a line-call was wrong, he would say so. But even if he conceded that point, it made the other player more reluctant to call another one out.'

He would not tolerate downright cheating, however, and would be quick to let his opponent know it.

John Brabban, who ran the tennis team with Lambert, remembers an incident in which Paul and a public schoolboy opponent were blatantly taunting each other over the net. At the change-over, the public schoolboy complained to his teacher.

'It turned out that Paul had called the boy to the net to tell him to stop making dodgy line-calls or Paul would shove his racket up his arse,' Mr Brabban says. 'When Paul saw that I was being told what had happened, he looked at me very sheepishly, but then got on with the game.

'But Paul was fair – sometimes too fair. He would play on when an opponent's shot was clearly out. And he was always generous in defeat – a good loser who never sulked.'

In school matches, Paul played against public schoolboys from wealthy backgrounds who turned out on court with pristine white tennis gear and £70 rackets. But, with his parents unable to afford some of the bare necessities of life, let alone white tennis gear, Paul had to play in his black Newcastle shorts, a white T-shirt and black trainers, and used his trusty old racket from the store room. It never seemed to bother him. When Paul represented Gateshead in the Coca-Cola National Schools Tennis League Championships, however, the rules insisted on competitors wearing white.

Jeff Lambert saved the day by lending Paul his kit – shirt, socks and shorts.

'The shirt and shorts were a bit big for him, but he was pleased with them and felt good,' Jeff remembers. 'The team got through to the last eight and I noticed Paul eyeing up my Nike basketball shoes. He had white trainers of his own by then, but fancied wearing mine, so I ended up lending him everything that day except my underpants.

'He didn't win that quarter-final, but put up a terrific fight and was competitive to the last shot.

'I know many teachers didn't care for him, but in the gym, or on the tennis court, he never did anything wrong and was nice to have around. I knew he could be a bit of a rascal, though, and he intrigued me during one match by going up to the net in between games to get something from a pile of clothes.

'I watched him do it a few times, then felt compelled to ask him what he was up to. He grinned cheekily and said he had some sweets hidden away. Thoughtfully, he asked me and a colleague if we'd like one. Noticing Paul reaching inside a sweaty sock inside one of his shoes, we graciously declined the offer!'

One Saturday afternoon the following September, Evan Bryson was watching Redheugh's Under-16 team play at home when he thought he recognized a boy standing on his own on the visiting supporters' side of the pitch.

He turned to Tommy Leonard, standing next to him, and pointed out the boy. 'Isn't that Gazza?' he said.

'Aye, it is,' Tommy said.

Evan kept looking at Paul, puzzled at why he hadn't come over to say hello. It was more than seven months since he had left, and the tension over John Gascoigne's deceit had long been forgotten.

Today, Evan recalls: 'Paul was obviously embarrassed and felt a bit humble. After the match, he started to walk away, so I caught up with him and said, "Hello there, Gazza, how are you?"

'"Oh, I'm okay thanks, Mr Bryson." He seemed a little bit down and slightly awkward, probably because he had never even said goodbye when he left us.

'"Where are you going now?" I asked.

'"Home," he said, a little forlornly.

'"Wouldn't you like to come back to the club and see all your friends?"

'Paul's face lit up. He was surprised. "Cann-ah?" he said in his broad Geordie.

'I said, "Of course you can – I certainly don't intend to cross the road whenever I see Paul Gascoigne because of what happened. We'd love you to come back and say hello."

'He was really pleased. He hopped in the back of the van with the other lads and we went back to the club. They all gave him a warm welcome, and it wasn't long before he was playing in the corridor and out in the yard and generally doing the things he loved doing before. It was like Paul had come home to us.

'He came back two or three times after that. It was good to see him again and it certainly made him feel very happy that we didn't think badly of him for what had happened. After all, we never blamed him for it.'

As the fifth and final year wore on, Paul continued to struggle with academic work. He did poorly in tests, and when the mock examinations were held to find out which O levels and CSEs he could take, his results were appalling; teachers felt he was not good enough to take even one O level. And the only CSE subjects they felt he had a chance in were English, environmental studies, and maths.

Paul was delighted.

If he was not going to take an exam in a subject, there was no point sitting in a classroom struggling to learn it, so he was allowed to drop out and do what he liked. Which, of course, was to play sport: tennis, basketball, general workouts in the gym, five-a-side football matches at lunchtime – anything, in fact, that was physical, not mental. The more subjects he had to drop, the better Paul liked it.

Jeff Lambert says: 'Paul was always being kicked out of classes, and would head straight for the gym. By the end of the term, he was a permanent fixture there!'

Paul once joked to John Brabban that he was so good at football because he had so much time on his hands to practise!

Mr Brabban says: 'A face would appear round the door of the gym and I'd say, "Who's that?"

'"It's Gascoigne, sir," he'd say. "I've been put out of History. Can I come and join you?"

'At that time, I was taking extra lessons to keep the

drop-outs occupied, so I'd always say yes, and he would come in and join a basketball class, or simply work out. He'd even join in a PE class with the first years.

'I loved having him around, because you always got fun from him. He had a ready smile and thoroughly enjoyed his sport. He was a kid I really hoped would do well.

'I never had any problems with him. He did get a bit over-excited at times, but I'd only have to threaten him with missing a game of football to bring a tear to his eye and make him step back in line.

'The rest of the kids loved him, too, because he would do the unorthodox. In tennis, he would spin the ball all over the court – even backhand top spin, which is one of the most difficult shots. And, in basketball, he would dribble and do fancy tricks with the ball, like bouncing it in and out of his legs.

'He was still a fighter, though, even in those games, and would never stop trying. He was an example to the others and if I saw anyone dropping their heads, I'd point to Paul and say, "Don't sulk. Get out there and do *that*."'

Every year from January until March, the football coach, Geoff Wilson, organized a boys against girls five-a-side tournament involving 200 pupils. The girls' teams had to have boys in goal, and vice versa. Girls in Paul's class would always want him to be their goalie because he was such a character. They loved his patter and found him funny.

Those games were a riot: the girls were given a ten-goal start and would try to stop the boys scoring by tripping them up and holding their shirts. Paul revelled in having a licence to play the clown and would have players and spectators alike in stitches as he dived all over the place or took the mickey out of the boys when he stopped them scoring. It would have been interesting if he had been allowed to lend a hand outfield, but he was not allowed to leave his goal.

Towards the end of that fifth year, Paul was good enough to be invited by teachers to join in their own five-a-side matches in the gym on Wednesday and Friday lunchtimes. And his amazing ability to 'nutmeg' – push the ball through an opponent's legs – soon became the sporting talk of the school.

Alan Cooke, an admiring victim of the Gascoigne wizardry, said: 'He would bring the ball up to me and I'd go to challenge, thinking I'd get the ball easily. But Paul would just play it straight through my legs in a flash. Or he would bounce it off the inside of my ankle and get the return ball, as if I'd meant it to go to him. It was only because he was so small that I was able to catch him and try to get the ball back.'

If he dribbled round Alan and went on to score, Paul would run back and wag a finger cheekily under Alan's nose, as if to say, 'Did you that time, sir.'

It was a habit that would infuriate and anger lads his own age when he played against them. He'd dribble round two or three players, go on to score, then run back, wagging his finger under their noses. They would lose their temper and try to stop him by running him into the wall. Paul knew he had won then, because they would mistime their challenges and he'd waltz round them even more easily. Bigger lads did catch him and sent him crashing at times but Paul never minded. He just picked himself up and got back in the game, always with a smile on his face.

'Paul was a tremendous footballer at school and I haven't seen anybody since with remotely near the same amount of skill,' Alan says. 'He was tiny, but his control was superb. He could do all kinds of things with the ball as if it was second nature.'

In June, a month after his sixteenth birthday, Paul sat his CSE exams. He did well enough in English and environmental studies to get low-grade passes, but it was the maths paper that summed up what, for him, had been a stunningly undistinguished academic year.

Predictably, he finished the exam early. And while the 250 other children in the school's sports hall had their heads down, deep in concentration, Paul began to feel bored. For something to do, he started fiddling with the wing nuts on his desk. It was probably the worst thing he could have done. The old wooden desk was in a bad state anyway and when Paul gave one twiddle too many it collapsed, shattering the heavy silence of the exam room and sending his exam papers fluttering to the floor. Paul managed to catch the desk top on his knees, but the loosened nuts and bolts went bouncing noisily along the floor.

All eyes turned on him. Some of the pupils giggled. The teacher at the front looked up angrily and demanded to know what the commotion was. Paul just sat there with the desk top on his lap and a silly grin on his face.

While other pupils tried to restore their concentration, Paul was ordered to re-assemble the desk. As one teacher said later: 'It was the hardest part of the exam for him, but the most successful.'

Certainly, it was typical of Paul at sixteen and seemed to sum up his feeling for maths.

He wanted only to play football for Newcastle and they were taking him on as an apprentice. You didn't need O levels to be a footballer, just great skill. And he had that in abundance. He was sure he could make it, and when his caring form master sounded a well-meaning warning, Paul's supreme confidence and self-belief provided the answer.

'You have to be realistic, Paul,' Mr Hepworth said. 'The chances of you becoming a professional footballer are few and far between. Only one in a thousand youngsters actually make it, you know.'

Paul gave the cheeky grin that Mr Hepworth had come to know so well over the last two years.

'Yes, I know,' Paul said. 'And that one will be me, sir.'

6

For a boy who wanted only to have a ball at his feet, the job of apprentice professional at Newcastle United was a daily nightmare for Paul.

He and the other apprentices were like servants to the coaching staff and senior professionals: any menial job that needed doing, they were expected to do it. They would have to ensure that playing kit was neatly laid out in the dressing rooms, at the training ground during the week and St James's Park on match days; they had to gather it up afterwards and stack it in a huge kit box. They had to sweep the dressing rooms and clean the toilets and showers. At the training sessions, they had to make sure balls and any other equipment were all at hand. And, of course, they had the privilege of cleaning the mud off senior professionals' boots.

To Paul, this was not what being a professional footballer was all about at all. He hated doing these jobs and he would do his best to get them done as quickly as possible, or to get out of them altogether. His lazy attitude did not endear him to Colin Suggett, a former Sunderland player, who was Newcastle's Youth Team coach, and his immediate boss.

Suggett quickly took a dislike to the self-assured, but work-shy, youngster. He certainly did not like his attitude to his job. He didn't like his practical jokes. He didn't like him being overweight. He didn't even seem to like his individual skill.

In that first year of his working life, Paul felt hounded by Suggett. If he failed to do a job properly – or ducked out of it altogether – the tough-talking coach would make him do press-ups, or clean out the toilets, as a punishment.

And when Paul got hold of a ball and started displaying the artistry he had been teaching himself since those childhood days in Teams, Suggett would sneer, 'If I wanted tricks, I'd get a clown from the circus.'

For Paul, the anguish of feeling persecuted could not have come at a more emotionally vulnerable time in his young life.

The deep scars left by Steven Spraggon's tragic death were slowly healing, but Paul still had his nervous stammer; and now, as he struggled to cope with the pressures of his first job, his father had walked out, leaving Carol Gascoigne with four children to bring up, and Paul was alone, confused and insecure.

He had never been shy to enjoy the warmth and friendliness of other families' homes; and now, with his own home life even more unsettled, Paul took on the role of gypsy more than ever.

Now that he had drifted apart from Keith Spraggon, he basked in the comradeship of the other apprentices, notably Paul Stephenson, Ian Bogie and Jeff Wrightson, whom he played against as a youngster; and when he went to their homes he found their parents as warm and welcoming as the Spraggons had been. They all took to the cheeky but well-mannered teenager and, hearing of his problems at home, they probably felt sorry for him too. Certainly, if Paul turned up out of the blue he would be offered something to eat and a bed for the night. He was made welcome at the Wrightson and Stephenson homes on more than one occasion, but Ian Bogie's parents felt particularly protective towards him and allowed him to move into their Crawford Terrace house, in Newcastle's Walker district. Eventually they gave Paul his own key and he and Ian became like brothers – even sleeping together in Ian's double bed.

The Bogies gave Paul a base and some stability at a time when he most needed it. Ian's father, Chick, even pretended to be Paul's dad once when a mix-up at a bank landed Paul in trouble with the manager. Paul had gone to a Newcastle branch of Barclays Bank to get some money from the cashpoint. He wanted £20, but, somehow, the machine interpreted the demand wrongly and pushed out £200. Unable to believe his luck, Paul went out and blew the money on a few nights out with his pals and a present for Ian's mother.

A few days later, however, bank staff discovered the error and the manager wrote to Paul, demanding that the money be repaid immediately. Too frightened to tell his mother, Paul confessed to Chick, who agreed to go to see the bank manager with him, posing as Paul's father. Knowing Paul was a Newcastle apprentice, the manager beamed when he heard Chick Bogie's broad Scottish accent. 'I didn't realize you were Scottish, Mr Gascoigne,' he said. 'So Paul will be able to play for Scotland, too!'

If that struck Paul and his bogus dad as amusing, the manager's next words did not. He appreciated that Paul had no money, but the bank would have to recover it from somewhere and, perhaps, start criminal proceedings for theft.

At that, Paul turned on the tears. And Chick played his part by giving him a clip round the ear and promising the manager that he would give Paul a good hiding when they got home.

The theatricals worked. Embarrassed by the scene, the manager said, 'I don't think there's any need for that, Mr Gascoigne. I'm sure we can sort this out in a way that won't upset Paul.'

He agreed to allow the money to be repaid in instalments Paul could afford and promised no further action if those payments were met. As 'father' and son walked out, Paul glanced at one of the cashiers and gave her a cheeky grin.

Where the Bogies could not help Paul was at work. And in those first six months of his Newcastle United life, Paul's football was in a mess.

In the early eighties, the club placed enormous emphasis

on defence, but Paul would not track back from midfield to pick up opposing players – and did not have the confidence to go forward, either. When he got the ball, his first thought was to run with it, but Suggett would order him to lay it off quickly to a team-mate. Paul was confused and became frightened of using his skill to dribble past opposing players in case he mucked it up and got a rollicking from Suggett. Consequently, Paul ended up playing in a restricted area, ten yards inside his own half and ten yards inside the opposition's.

For a boy who had dreamed of entertaining the crowds in the terraces, it was unbearable. For Colin Suggett it was intolerable. And, with the club's best interests at heart, he cracked down with a toughness that Paul found hard to take.

Worrying made him unhappy, and he began to lose confidence until eventually he became frightened that Newcastle would not keep him on and he would have to look for another way to earn a living, his football dreams over. The fear turned him into something of a nervous wreck and suddenly the screech he made when he forced himself to swallow turned into a sort of bark. One of Newcastle's backroom staff would invite Paul round for Sunday lunch and the whole meal would be interrupted constantly by Paul's embarrassing bark and stutter. He would admit that he was worried sick about his future in the game.

The stutter and bark were apparent, too, in the dressing room before Saturday matches in the Northern Intermediate League. Paul's opponents were other apprentice professionals, but they were up to three years older and stronger, and the games were extremely gruelling and physically tough. Paul would sit there, waiting to go out, ridiculously tense, worrying about his personal life, his career, and if he was going to do what was expected of him on the pitch.

What did not help in those early days was his nomadic lifestyle. With no one at home to provide a regular wholesome meal, Paul would rely on junk food to get him through the day; and, of course, if he popped into a friend's home unexpectedly, he would be given a quick meal of egg, sausages and chips. He had always been on the tubby side, and now, at sixteen, he got tubbier.

If Suggett was not happy with a lazy Paul, he was furious with a lazy, fat Paul. For the boy who had dreamed of a Newcastle playing career, the reality became a nightmare. Paul became so distressed, so worried at what lay ahead, that he would walk to the iron gates of the Benwell training ground from the bus and stop, thinking, 'I can't face going through.' For he knew that in the changing rooms, at the end of 150 yards of ash track, Suggett was waiting for him, and he did not know if he could take it.

Joe Harvey, a Newcastle captain in the fifties, who became assistant manager, then chief scout, was alive then. And Paul would go back to St James's Park after training to open his heart to him and Peter Kirkley.

'There's no doubt about it, Paul dreaded facing Suggett,' Kirkley says today. 'He'd be in tears, all crumpled up. At first, Joe and I thought he was putting it on to get our sympathy because we knew he had only his mum at home, and needed someone to listen to him. But we quickly realized the lad was distressed.

'We'd ask what was the matter, and Paul would complain that Suggett had been picking on him again, calling him 'fatty' and telling him off for not doing his jobs. He felt Suggett was singling him out and making him look a fool.

'We told Paul he had only himself to blame if he didn't do his work properly. He knew what he was expected to do, so he should just go out and do it.

'But when Paul started on the football side, that was a different matter and I wanted to know what was going wrong. It had puzzled me why good young schoolboys I had brought in had not improved. Even with Paul, I'd seen a change. I'd watch him play for Dunston Juniors on a Sunday and see him dribble past players and score great goals. But, like others, he wasn't producing the same form now he was full-time.

'It bothered me that potentially good schoolboys were suddenly being released at eighteen and I wondered why.'

Kirkley says he had put it down to natural wastage. But, after listening to Paul – and two other apprentices, Bogie and Wrightson – he realized the problem was deeper than that. Suggett's coaching method seemed to restrict the flair player, the dribbler who could create goal-scoring chances by doing the unexpected and unorthodox.

Kirkley says: 'Paul had told me he wanted freedom to express himself, to show off his skill and entertain. But all Suggett wanted him to do was run up and down the pitch, laying the ball off quickly to a colleague, and making sure he was always marking an opponent when the team didn't have the ball.

'When I work with boys of ten and eleven with another coach, Stan Nixon, they are always told not to be frightened to ask questions if they don't understand what we're asking them to do. But Paul and the other lads were being treated like robots, not able to think for themselves.

'Paul wasn't the type to be miserable, despite his personal problems, and he would get up to all sorts of pranks, like hiding other players' clothes or tying their tracksuit bottoms together, so they couldn't get their feet in. They were harmless jokes, without any hint of malice, but Suggett could never accept that. He wanted players who never questioned anything, only did what they were told, and never did anything out of the ordinary. He just could not comprehend that Paul was not like everyone else, but an individual who liked to be different and do different things.'

Today, Suggett freely admits that Paul was a thorn in his side.

'He drove me mad,' he says. 'I had more problems with him than with all the other apprentices put together. If he could sneak out of something, sweep the dirt under the carpet, or whatever, he would. I'd have to be chasing his tail all the time. He was so disruptive, too – always playing the fool and larking around behind my back and making the other lads laugh.

'When he got into trouble, he turned on the tears to make you feel sorry for him. I heard him boasting to the other apprentices how he did it. They were all in the bath and I crept up and said, "Oh, aye, Gazza – that's very clever." He was very embarrassed.

'Outside the club, he was into all sorts of things he shouldn't have been. And, quite honestly, in that first year, I wondered if a football career meant enough to him to get down and work at it.'

As that first year wore on, Kirkley became increasingly concerned about Paul. Some of his jauntiness was being knocked out of him and Kirkley began to notice the nervous behaviour.

'He would get rid of one affliction, then another would start,' says Kirkley. 'When his barking stopped, I'd say, "You've got rid of the dog, then, Paul." By then, he had developed another nervous habit – a dry cough, or something. I don't think he knew he was doing it. He had various mild afflictions, which came on whenever he was anxious or tense. Other lads used to take the mickey and mimic him.'

And then one morning after training, Paul broke down and cried and told Kirkley he couldn't take it any more. He wanted to chuck it in at Newcastle and go somewhere else.

Kirkley knew he had to confront Suggett.

'What is it about Paul that offends you?' Kirkley asked. 'What makes you so aggressive towards him?'

Suggett told him that Paul was always playing the fool and never doing what he was told.

Kirkley suggested that he was going about it the wrong way; that, perhaps, he should treat Paul more as an individual. But Suggett insisted he was not doing anything wrong.

The confrontation ended with Kirkley angrily telling Suggett to lay off Paul and to try to handle him better, because he was driving the lad away.

Today, Kirkley is still angry. 'We have players at Newcastle who could be as good as Paul, but I fear the coaching attitude is in danger of killing off the talent. Someone should be behind the skilful lads, saying, "Ignore what they're telling you and keep going."

'Being responsible for bringing in talented schoolboys, I naturally want the best treatment for them, and I take it personally if they're treated badly. I don't like the way Suggett treats the lads.

'Certainly his approach could have finished Paul. We had an enormous amount to do in this club to keep the boy going, to keep doing his tricks.

'It wouldn't have bothered Suggett if Paul had quit, because he didn't like his attitude and appeared to want him out. But it would have been terrible for everyone else here, and for Paul himself. The only dream he had was to go out in the black and white of Newcastle and entertain the fans.'

Between them, Harvey and Kirkley boosted Paul's morale and kept him going that terrible year. When Paul would worry about doing things wrong in a game and getting on the wrong side of Suggett, Joe, the old Newcastle favourite, would say: 'What does he know about football, Paul? When a game kicks off, he has no control over you, so do what *you* want to do.'

Kirkley, too, advised him not to conform. 'To get by in life,' he'd say, 'you have to be who you are and what you are; you must not allow yourself to be changed.'

Kevin Keegan was playing for Newcastle then and Paul had to clean his boots; he had even taken a new pair home to break in and had lost one on the underground train to Gateshead. Keegan was something of a hero, particularly to young apprentices, and they all wanted to be like him. But Kirkley stressed to Paul: 'Don't copy anybody – even Kevin. Be yourself. Always.'

Paul possibly looked on Harvey and Kirkley as father figures. He listened carefully to what they told him and then, with the same fighting spirit and will to win he had shown throughout his hard upbringing, he went through the gates of the training ground and up the long, forbidding ash track, to the changing rooms, determined not to be crushed by Suggett's strict and unforgiving régime.

And then, in June, shortly after Paul's seventeenth birthday, Newcastle announced they were appointing a new manager to replace Arthur Cox. His name was Jack Charlton.

What effect, the troubled teenager wondered, would the big man have on his future?

7

One of the most important and early jobs for a new manager is to assess his playing staff. And when Jack Charlton heard about Paul, he was far from impressed. Suggett told him the boy was a disruptive influence and he did not care enough about the game. It might be in the club's interests, he advised Jack, to let him go.

Jack immediately went to Joe Harvey and Peter Kirkley and told them that Suggett had given him a run-down on what a bad character Paul was and the terrible things he got up to.

Kirkley remembers the day well. 'Joe shook his head and said, "Gazza's not a bad lad – he's just mischievous and a little bit hard to handle."

'I stepped in and corrected him. "Hard to handle for Suggett, you mean. Gazza doesn't give *us* any bother."

'Jack wasn't convinced. He said he would have him up to his office and have it out with him. Joe and I were very worried. "If you let him go, Jack," we said, "you'll be getting rid of the best talent we've got."'

Several days later, Gazza came up the stairs and stood outside Jack's office in his tracksuit, waiting to be called in. Kirkley and Harvey knew Jack was a hard man who stood no nonsense and they feared the worst. They felt Jack was going to go for Gazza with everything he had.

But after about seven minutes the big man came out of his office, looking close to tears.

Kirkley recalls: 'Jack said, "Can you get us two cups of coffee, please. The lad's crying in there." Then he shook his head, sadly. "What a life he's had."

'Joe said, "From the look of you, I think you're going to cry and all." "Well," Jack said, "he *has* had a rough time."'

Whether it had finally dawned on Gazza that his bad behaviour and general stupidity had finally caught up with him, only he knows. But he turned on the tears for Jack Charlton that day. Fearing that he might be kicked out the door, his football dreams over, he appealed to the sympathetic side of Big Jack's tough nature.

It was true: he *had* had a tough life, and his parents had split up. But Gazza piled on the agony very thickly for Jack that day.

And Jack bought it.

Kirkley says: 'I don't know exactly what Gazza said, but he needed only to talk about his dad running off with someone else, and his mum being left on her own at home, and Jack would have been moved. He's very soft-hearted.'

Jack was not *that* soft-hearted, however. When he went back into his office, he made it clear that Gazza was getting only a short reprieve. He had just three weeks to lose a stone and generally get his act together – or he was out the door.

Jack's main concern, according to Kirkley, was Gazza's

unhealthy eating habits; he knew the lad wasn't living at home and never ate regularly or well.

'I will make sure he gets at least one good, sensible meal a day,' Jack said. He arranged for Gazza to eat a specially prepared lunch at the club's expense – about £12 a week – at the Oven Door, a small restaurant run by reliable people, a couple of miles from the training ground.

Gazza walked out of Jack Charlton's office that August morning in a state of shock.

The big man had laid it on the line that, for him at least, supreme artistry with a football was not enough to guarantee a future in the game; he had made Gazza realize, perhaps for the first time in his young life, that all those boyhood dreams of playing in the famous black and white Magpie shirt could be over before they had begun. And over in three weeks. Over at the age of seventeen!

Gazza realized he had been pulled back from the brink and given a chance. He also knew that, if he blew it, there would not be another one.

Now he had a choice – a heartbreakingly tough but simple one: either he knuckled down, lost weight, cut out the clowning and behaved like the pro he wanted to be; or he called Jack Charlton's bluff and risked the sack, and all the disappointment and humiliation that would go with it.

Gazza decided to knuckle down.

He threw himself into Suggett's morning training sessions with a new zest, a new will. And after his specially prepared meal at the Oven Door he went back to the Benwell ground and sweated it out still more under Suggett's watchful eye. The coach was still tough, still demanding; but he was more of an ally now, not an adversary, and Gazza responded to his urgings with all the sporting determination he had shown throughout his life. He'd always wanted to be a winner at the only thing he could do well; and now he wanted to be a winner, the very best, more than ever. He ran and sweated, and when he was exhausted and wanting to rest, he thought of the chance he'd been given, and pushed himself some more. Slowly, the treacherous pounds started to disappear.

'Gazza knew it was make or break and really worked hard,' says Suggett. 'He came to training in the morning, then came back in the afternoons. He pushed himself and gave 100 per cent, no matter how hard I was with him. But, then, he had never cheated at training. I had no complaints there.'

He didn't cheat at the Oven Door, either.

Sue Thompson, a partner in the restaurant, said, 'Before Jack Charlton introduced the diet, Paul would come in with the other lads and tuck into lasagne and loads of chips. But not once during the time he was on our diet did he ask for chips. He took it very seriously indeed.

'He was very quiet and seemed shy when he came in. He just sat in a corner, either on his own or with a friend. I can't remember having to tell him off for being noisy or fooling around.

'He didn't know what he was eating until he came in, but usually it was sirloin steak with salad. We tried fish one day, but Paul didn't like it and he never had it again.'

Peter Kirkley stepped in and lent a hand, too. Fed up with the knockers saying Gazza was a carthorse who could not run, he suggested extra work under Brendan Foster's coach, Stan Long, at Gateshead Stadium. If Stan was interested, would Gazza go there, Kirkley wanted to know. The boy said he would.

'As long as I picked him up and he knew I was watching, he worked,' says Kirkley. 'He slogged it out with some of the athletes and slowly built up his stamina.

'Then another local athlete, Harry Plant, tried to help Gazza with his sprinting. But it was all too intricate, more about technique, and Gazza didn't need that. Anything was worth trying at that time, though.

'People were also saying Gazza looked awkward and wasn't balanced. So I asked a balance expert called Lenny Hepple to study Gazza. He said there was nothing wrong with the lad's balance – in fact he was perfect. He asked me to watch how Gazza leaned back then exploded past people, and he explained that Gazza gets power by using his weight to his best advantage.'

By Christmas 1984, Gazza had changed dramatically. The flabbiness had been replaced by muscle, and he had suddenly shot up by two or three inches. The loss of weight, with the extra height, made him look fitter, sharper and more powerful. And in youth team matches his new-found strength, speed and stamina lifted his performance.

'He was miles behind physically in his first year, but he was a different fella in the second,' says Suggett. 'He could go by players at will and was strong enough to hold them off.'

Paul may not have been the brainiest boy at school, but, according to Suggett, he had a shrewdness that enabled him to get the best out of people and work out short-cuts in almost everything he did. He was a clever player and a clever person, able to manipulate people, and in sport he was bright and a very quick learner.

'At first, Gazza was very ordinary in pace, but he got the hang of shuttle-runs in no time, and from being the slowest he became the fastest,' says Suggett. 'He was streetwise, and worked out how he could gain a yard every time he turned. If he could see a short-cut in something he always took it and got there before anybody else.

'From early on, he was exciting in that he could do things other lads couldn't do, like chip the keeper regularly from twenty-five yards. But the weight was always a prob-lem. He was always flitting from here to there, never in his own house, never eating the right food. I was always on to him. I had to be. He would never have lost it otherwise.'

Off the field, Gazza's attitude to his job as an apprentice had not changed. Whatever he was told to do, he did quickly and he did not care if it was done well.

'Gazza hated everything, but no more than any of the others,' says Suggett. 'I told him that jobs wouldn't go away – the fairies didn't come in and do them. But I'd still find him in the gym with a ball and his job not done. I'd be chasing him all the time.'

Gazza had another worry about being chased that season – by 'Mad Max', the dog at the training ground. The groundsman, David Orchard, got the ten-month-old long-haired alsatian from the RSPCA following some break-ins – and it quickly became the scourge of the players. Only David, his wife and children and the night-watchman could handle the dog; everyone else was terrified and would not go near him.

'Max was so fierce we had to ask the RSPCA to find him a new owner,' says David. 'He was always biting players, and once he nipped a young fan who had come to watch the lads train.

'Max would always scratch the door of his cage to be let out and Gazza would think it fun to slip the lock when no one was watching. Someone let Max out one morning while the first team were out on the field training. I've never seen the players run so fast. The cry went out: "The dog's out!" and everybody started running wildly in all directions. All, that is, except one of the coaches, John Pickering. Max was heading straight for him and John was so scared, he just stood like a statue in the middle of the field, not daring to move. Someone had the presence of mind to kick a football in front of it to distract the dog's attention for a moment. John and everyone else sprinted towards the changing rooms and someone slammed the door shut – with Max inches from John's backside.'

At this time, Paul's ability was exciting many people at the club. One person more excited than most was Jackie Milburn, the former Newcastle centre forward, who played thirteen times for England. Before one match at St James's Park, he went up to England manager Bobby Robson in the directors' lounge and said, 'We've got a lad coming through the juniors, Bob. His name is Gascoigne – and he's going to be great.'

They were prophetic words that Robson would have

cause to remember on another visit to the ground before Milburn's death in October 1988.

If being an apprentice professional footballer was not all that he expected it to be, the job did hold one huge attraction for Paul.

In the promotions' office at St James's Park, just a free-kick from the main entrance, there are three smartly dressed, middle-aged women who run the club's fund-raising lottery. The women have a cheery outlook on life and their office is popular among Newcastle United staff: there are constant comings and goings and a general hubbub of pleasant chit-chat and jovial banter. Once he had discovered that happy office, the friendliness of those women, Margaret Tickle, Maureen Ashcroft and Madeline Grahame, drew him like a magnet and he found any excuse to pop in for a chat and bask in the warmth of their bubbly personalities.

The office was a place where he could go any time of the day when he had nothing to do, nowhere to go and no one to see; a place where he felt comfortable and he belonged; where he would be welcomed, perhaps be given a cup of tea and something to eat, by people he liked and who liked him.

With no one likely to be at home in Dunston, Paul would make for that office around midday after training, and stay chatting for two, maybe three, hours, sometimes even longer.

If he was playing in an evening match, he'd go to the office as early as 5 p.m. and sit there drinking coffee until 6.45 before he went to the dressing room. It got to a point where, if he didn't arrive, one of the women would ask, 'Where's Paul?'

He confided in those women in a way he probably had not confided in anybody in his life. He told them his problems, revealed secrets, asked their advice, moaned about his job, even talked about sex. Indeed, at the club they were known as Paul's 'mums' who were keeping an affectionate, maternal eye on his welfare.

Margaret, Maureen and Madeline revelled in their roles.

'He led us a merry dance one way and another, but he was a lovely lad and we thought the world of him,' they all agree today. 'We knew he didn't have much of a home life – much of anything, in fact – so we took care of him and tried to make sure he was as happy as possible.'

One of the main problems in those early apprenticeship years was money: Paul earned only £20 a week and, more often than not, would be broke long before pay day. He quickly learned that in the three kindly lottery ladies he had a friendly financial arm on which he could lean.

'We were always lending Paul money – and willingly so,' says Margaret. 'He always paid us back, though – every penny. We knew when he wanted something; he'd move along to the end of the counter in our office and make funny faces at us, or attract one of us with a quiet "Psst". Usually he wanted a tenner or so to last him till the end of the week, but there were times when he asked for more. Once, he was going on holiday and hadn't been able to save any spending money, so we cashed a cheque and gave him £100. He was very grateful and repaid it in instalments when he got back.

'We all remember the time Paul went on a club tour of Fiji. We gave him an envelope as he was about to leave and made him promise not to open it till he was away from the ground. It was only £40 or so we'd put together but we felt it might come in handy, especially if he wanted to buy the lads some drinks at the airport and on the plane. Paul appreciated it and when he came home – a little early because he was homesick – he brought us all a little present each.'

Having little money did not make Paul stingy, however. In those days, it seems, he was always treating people he did not know to drinks, even if he could not afford to. Once, at a Saturday night gathering in Dunston's Excelsior Working Men's Club, he insisted on buying a huge round. The following Monday he went to the lottery office, a little embarrassed. 'Those drinks on Saturday have left me a bit short,' he confessed to the friendly trio. 'Couldn't lend us a tenner until Friday, could you?'

Another time, at a twenty-first birthday, he was at a table with comparative strangers and about to put his hand in his pocket for a large round. Maureen's husband went over and offered to pay, but Paul insisted on doing it himself. He had a certain working-class pride in paying his way, even if it was not always easy to do so.

Paul had the most inane, childish sense of humour which, had he been less likeable, well-meaning and not so promising a footballer, would surely have got him the sack or, at the very least, a punch on the nose.

Noticing him eyeing the fire-alarm button in the office one day, Maureen warned him to leave it alone. But, like a bored and naughty child looking to get into mischief, he pressed it defiantly, setting off a deafening bell all around the main entrance. Another time he grabbed a fire extinguisher off the wall and ran out, squirting foam all over the car park.

'He was just plain daft and stupid,' all three women agree. 'And it's a wonder he didn't get into a lot more trouble than he did.'

They were all protective to Paul, as one might expect, and when he ran into their office for safety after perpetrating some devilish prank elsewhere in the ground, they would hide him in a back room and deny his presence to whichever club official rushed in wanting his blood.

Paul, no doubt, enjoyed this adult version of hide-and-seek, not so much for the fun of it, but because the room he hid in had a kettle, teapot and all kinds of refreshment. When the coast was clear, one of the women would open the door to find Paul sitting there, scoffing a cake or sandwich. Not an ideal situation for someone constantly fighting the flab!

In those carefree apprenticeship years, Paul's 'mums' saw another side of his personality which, if anything, endeared him to them every more. It was his emotional nature; he could – and often would, if it suited him – burst into tears at the least little thing that upset him.

'If he was told off in training for not pulling his weight, the chances are that he'd turn on the waterworks,' says Margaret. 'He'd even start crying when one of us got fed up with all his stupidness and told him to get lost. He was a very, very emotional lad and things got to him more than the other lads. Don't ask me why. He seemed a lonely lad at times, all right, but he was happy enough. And no sooner was he down in the mouth and crying than he'd be up again, enjoying a joke.'

In spite of the cavalier laugh-a-minute attitude he presented to his 'mums' in their homely base, it is fair to say that Paul's apprenticeship was not the happiest time of his life. He wanted to be a footballer, not skivvy to older professionals; he wanted to show off his skills with the ball, not clean toilets. And the only sweeping he had any interest in went on in a team's defence, not in the dressing room.

Gazza's new-found strength and stamina helped him put together a string of fine performances for the youth team; and, in training, senior pros started telling him it wouldn't be long before he forced himself into the first-team squad. Gazza could not control his cockiness in five-a-side games, however, and upset players so much that some threatened to thump him. Slimmer, fitter and stronger than before, he was bubbling with confidence, able to hold his own with anyone, and he would love to take the ball up to a first-teamer, 'nutmeg' him, and shout 'Legs' as he ran past, laughing loudly.

'It was wonderful to watch,' David Orchard recalls. 'But the senior pros would go berserk at being humiliated by a young kid not yet in the first team. Several certainly tried to chop him and a few others wanted to give him a right-hander to bring him down a peg.'

Kirkley, however, insists this was just the impish side of Gazza.

'All good ball players have a certain amount of arrogance, but his mickey-taking was more out of mischief,' he says. 'Gazza never went out to humiliate people. He would have seen it as a bit of a giggle. I do know the pros didn't see it that way, though. They did try to lame him in those games, but he was too quick.'

Gazza was playing well for the juniors, but he was still far from happy with the restricted role he was being asked to play. He wanted more freedom to express himself. He wanted to entertain, and he felt his talent to do so was being muzzled.

In his despair, Peter Kirkley says, Paul would go to Joe Harvey's office and pour it all out. Joe would again advise him to play his own game. Kirkley says: 'Joe would say, "Sod Suggett, whatever he says. If he starts yelling at you for doing something he doesn't like, give him a wave and the thumbs up and carry on playing your own game."'

Gazza did just that. He got a lot of stick from the dugout and more of it at half-time, but, by then, he had started to realize he was making an impact on the terraces; fans appreciated what he was doing and were starting to take notice of him.

He was not sure if the club were going to sign him as a full-time professional at the end of his two years, however. Despite his dedication in training, he knew he was not the flavour of the month; and if Suggett had anything to do with it, he probably would not get a contract.

And then, surprisingly, on 13 April, Jack Charlton named Gazza as a sub for the home game against QPR. With twenty minutes left, the lad got the nod and ran proudly, if nervously, on to the St James's Park pitch for his first-team debut ... just forty-four days before his eighteenth birthday.

The best present Gazza could have wished for was a

contract to be a full-time professional with Newcastle United. But no one was saying anything. His future, it seemed, was still undecided. Gazza did not have time to dwell on it, however, because the following Tuesday he was playing in the first leg of the FA Youth Cup Final against Watford at St James's.

What had promised to be a glorious end to an exciting Youth Cup run looked like ending in disappointment when Watford defended brilliantly to earn a 0–0 draw and started favourites in the second leg at Watford on 10 May.

Whether Gazza was still on a high from that brief first-team appearance is not clear. Maybe he just sensed that his career hung in the balance and this one high-profile game could tip the scales in his favour. What *is* certain is that on that Friday night he was inspired. He ran all over the park. He brought team-mates into the game with exquisite passing. He made telling forward runs and funnelled back to help out in defence. He ran the show.

And he guided Newcastle to a scintillating 4–1 victory to lift the FA Youth Cup for the first time in the club's history.

It was a magical night and his 'mums' Margaret and Maureen remember it well.

'Knowing Gazza's parents wouldn't be making such a long trip, we decided to go to the game to give him support,' says Margaret. 'He was absolutely brilliant and it would be nice to think we helped, in some small way, to raise his game that night by being his "family" for a while.

'It was an emotional occasion for all of us and I'll never forget Gazza coming on to the supporters' coach before we headed home. He was holding the cup so proudly – and crying his eyes out.'

If the Newcastle management *had* been uncertain about Gazza, that performance convinced them that he was a star of the future. As Peter Kirkley says, 'He was so outstanding they couldn't get his signature fast enough.'

And after Gazza had signed a two-year contract with a

two-year option, Jack Charlton remembered that three-week ultimatum with a certain ruefulness.

'I've made some bad mistakes,' he admitted. 'But getting rid of Gazza would have been the worst mistake of my life.'

8

Shortly after five o'clock on the evening of Saturday 10 August, 1985, one week before the start of the new soccer season, crisis hit Newcastle United.

Jackie Charlton walked out.

Throughout a friendly with Sheffield United at St James's Park, Geordie fans had been screaming, 'We hate you, Charlton . . .' and 'Jack must go.' After the final whistle, the fifty-year-old World Cup winning defender went to see the Newcastle chairman, Stan Seymour, to grant them their wish.

Later, he told his uncle, Jackie Milburn, who was covering the match for a Sunday newspaper, 'I need that like a hole in the head.'

Charlton, who had been the manager for just fourteen months, had angered fans, starved of success, by failing to buy a star replacement for Chris Waddle, failing to agree personal terms with former Ipswich striker Eric Gates, who subsequently signed for rivals Sunderland, and failing to persuade Peter Beardsley to sign a new contract.

With the new season only days away, Jackie's shock walkout put the Newcastle board in a difficult position, and they had little option but to promote Willie McFaul to acting manager.

Willie knew a lot about Gazza. He had seen him arrive at the club's training ground the day after he left school. He knew he was a chirpy lad with boundless skill; but he was also aware the lad was a mischievous rascal who preferred to play, not work. The school had warned Willie about Gazza's behaviour. Even in those early days, Willie felt like clipping Gazza round the ear every time he passed.

'I knew that if he wasn't going to trouble, he would be coming from it,' says Willie.

Gazza's progress in the juniors, however, had impressed Willie. There was still a lot wrong in the lad's game, but he seemed to be learning when to use his skill and when not to. His form in the youth team's cup run had been a joy to watch. And his performance in the final . . . well, that was quite breathtaking.

When Willie moved into the St James's Park hot seat, he knew for sure that Gazza would feature in his plans. The question was when – and how? He could play safe: perhaps make Gazza a sub and bring him on for the last ten minutes of a few games; not long enough for Gazza to get in the game, express himself as much as he might like, but it would, at least, acclimatize him to the pace of the First Division; and sitting on the subs' bench as one of the squad would be good for his confidence.

Another option for Willie could be to leave Gazza out of his first team plans altogether and see how the senior pros began the season; playing for the reserves for a while might be good for the lad anyway, keeping his feet on the ground for a while after all that Youth Cup acclaim.

In the end, Willie did neither. He had a good feeling about the lad. Gazza was barely past his eighteenth birthday, but the effort he'd put into his pre-season training had almost matched his exceptional skill on the ball. His fitness was right, and so, it seemed, was his attitude. On the journey down to Southampton on the Friday before the game, Willie knew what he had to do. But he didn't tell anyone. He named his squad, then told Gazza he was taking him on the trip to take care of the kit: it would be valuable experience for him. Gazza was thrilled.

The following day, the squad had an early pre-match meal in a hotel outside Southampton.

Afterwards, Willie pulled Gazza to one side.

'How do you feel?' he asked gently.

In a small nervous voice, Gazza replied, 'I feel all right. I feel all right.'

'I'm playing you today, son,' said Willie.

Gazza stared at him, wide-eyed with surprise. Then he smiled.

'Thanks, boss,' he said. 'I'll not let you down.'

Today, Willie recalls: 'I knew we didn't have many worries. Gazza was delighted, really chuffed. I felt we just had to get him to do the things we wanted him to, and everything would be all right.

'I'm sure Gazza had no idea I was going to play him. I hadn't mentioned it to anyone – not even Colin Suggett. Gazza is an excitable lad and was always nervy and uptight before matches. I wanted to keep the pressure off him for as long as I could.

'There wasn't one particular moment when I thought: he's ready – I'm going to play him. I knew he had that explosive talent and it was only a question of channelling it in the right way. I could have brought him on as a sub late in the game, but I felt we had to start with him. I certainly had the confidence in him to give him a go and see what he could do. If the match had been at St James's Park I may have thought differently, because there would have been far more pressure on him. But a game a long way from home was ideal for both of us.'

Gazza, who played in midfield with David McCreery, was warned to keep things simple when he picked up the ball from the back four – and take players on and show off his tricks *only* in Southampton's third of the field. Gazza obeyed Willie's orders and was playing well in a good all-round Newcastle performance when, nine minutes from the end, Willie nudged Suggett in the dugout.

'Get Gazza off,' he said.

Suggett was shocked. 'You can't take him off.'

'Get him off,' Willie insisted. 'I can see something happening that might spoil his whole day. And ours, too.'

The next time the ball went out of play, Suggett called Gazza off the pitch. The reaction among the few thousand Newcastle fans who had made the trip south was fierce: cheers for Gazza's performance, jeers for Willie taking him off. Gazza, himself, hated being pulled off: he knew he was playing well and was enjoying himself. As he reached the dugout, Willie just said, 'You've done enough, and you've done well.'

And today, Willie still feels he made the right decision.

'I wasn't being selfish,' he says. 'As a manager, you get certain feelings. We were drawing 1–1 and were happy to go home with a point. I'd been impressed with Gazza on the day, but near the end I could see he was beginning to get cocky. Now, I love that in a player, but there has to be a right time to show off, and it was not then, not at such a crucial stage of the game. The Newcastle fans gave me a lot of stick because they were enjoying watching Gazza. But, in the end, I don't think taking him off did him any harm.'

Having seen the way Gazza grabbed his chance, it would have been easy for Willie to pencil in the boy's name for the first team every week. Certainly the Newcastle fans had been starved of such virtuosity for years and would have welcomed it. But Willie was too experienced and wise in the footballing world not to foresee possible dangers. Worried that such a young and relatively immature kid would become blasé and not appreciate what was happening to him, Willie decided not to play Gazza every week but to nurse him along instead.

They were difficult days, both for the boy himself and the senior professionals who admired his talent and were looking after him.

'He was just a young lad and, like every other young lad, he wanted to enjoy himself,' McFaul says. 'But, in such a fanatical football city as Newcastle, the fans quickly put a brilliant young player on a pedestal where he can do no wrong. And, unless the discipline is there, he can be tempted to get into bad habits. I'd seen talent in others fall by the way-side and I was determined it wouldn't happen to Gazza.

'We had good pros at the club – Glenn Roeder, David McCreery, Paul Goddard, particularly – and they all went out of their way to help Gazza and make him appreciate what the game was all about,' says Willie. 'Sometimes Gazza reacted against it. He could stick up for himself against any pro, but sometimes he got a bit carried away with himself and there was the odd blow-up. They all had to keep at him and convince him their way was right. They didn't have his talent, but they had the other bit – the discipline. And this is what Gazza needed, too, in those early days.'

Eating was the biggest problem. With no one on his back to insist on him having a regular balanced meal, Paul slipped back into bad habits, making do with junk food. This, in turn, put on those dreaded surplus pounds and incurred the wrath of McFaul and Suggett, who made him run round in bin liners to help him sweat.

'We all remember him having a tough time training,' Margaret Tickle says. 'But he'd still stroll in an hour or so later and start tucking into the fish and chips we'd got in for our lunch. He'd have chocolate biscuits, Mars bars and munchmallows, too, saying as he ate them, "I shouldn't be eating these. I've put so much weight on and I've got to get it off." '

He still kept eating junk food, though – sometimes just to prove a point and show his independence. Once, one of the Newcastle staff saw Paul playing pool and generally hanging around at a sports complex, and warned him that Suggett had been going on about his weight again. Paul was furious. He was sick of people nagging him about his weight, he said, and turned to a young friend, called Sammy and gave him 50p. 'Go off and get me some sweets,' he said. 'As many as you can for that.' When

Sammy came back with fifty one-penny liquorice chews, Paul pulled a face. 'Well, I don't like those too much,' he said. Then he grinned. 'But I'll eat them anyway.'

Just why Paul continued to put his career at risk by eating food he knew was bad for him is a mystery. Perhaps it was due to a lack of parental guidance and generally unsettled home life; perhaps, with money always tight, it had become a way of life for Paul to seize whatever food was available whenever he had the chance.

Or, perhaps, it was because he was daft. Just plain stupid.

Certainly, Margaret, Maureen and Madeline all agree that Paul is the stupidest person they have met. And, judging by the antics he got up to, the label is more than justified.

Having left school with just those two CSEs, his knowledge was extraordinarily modest, and he would reduce his 'mums' to helpless laughter at some of the things he said.

Once, he told Maureen that he sometimes got fed up having to sign autographs at certain places.

'You should go incognito,' Maureen suggested, helpfully.

Paul looked at her blankly for a few seconds, then asked innocently, 'Where's cognito?'

Another time, when there was a football story in one of the papers involving Monaco, Maureen said, 'I bet you don't know where Monaco is.'

Paul shook his head and muttered something that seemed to indicate he didn't.

'Don't you know of Prince Rainier?' Maureen asked.

'Nah,' Paul replied. Then he grinned and joked, 'But I bet he knows who I am.'

Another time, after Paul had inquired whether he needed his passport for Scotland, Maureen was prompted to say, 'Just as well you've got feet that can kick a ball, my lad, 'cos you've got nowt up top.'

'Ah, shut up, ya old biddy,' Paul replied cheekily.

Exasperated, Maureen waved him away. 'Go on now, get out, get lost.'

'Right, that's it,' Paul would say. And he'd walk out the door, saying, 'I'm not coming back.'

But the next day he'd walk in the office as if nothing had happened, and greet the women cheerily. 'Hi, lassies.'

'Thought you weren't coming back,' Maureen would say. But Paul would just laugh.

Nothing, it seems, would keep him down for long. He always had a positive, almost cavalier, attitude to even the most serious issue. After Paul had been in trouble with the coaching staff for misbehaving, Maureen warned him: 'If you don't behave, you'll be on the scrapheap, without a job and no money.'

Unruffled, Paul replied immediately. 'Well, I'll be a bin man, 'cos I love the fresh air.'

The wage increase he got from being a first-teamer meant that Paul now had more money than at any time in his life. And he wasted no time spending it. Never having been able to afford smart, new clothes before, Paul would go on spending sprees in Newcastle, then proudly show his purchases to his admirers in the lottery office.

'And it always struck us as odd that whenever he showed us a new jacket or suit, or whatever, he'd always tell us how much he'd paid for it,' says Margaret. 'Money was so, so important to him, because he'd never had any in his life. He couldn't wait to spend it and he'd go out and buy anything that took his fancy. He even bought an organ once!'

Nowhere was Paul's immaturity more evident than in the sexual banterings and boastings he indulged in with the three women old enough to be his mother. He would talk candidly about alleged sexual conquests and make suggestive remarks. To Margaret, for example, he would say, 'Is your husband out? Do you fancy it? Just tell me when he's out and I'll be round.'

Once, he put his hand up Maureen's skirt and discovered she was wearing suspenders. 'After that,' she says, 'he'd always be saying, "Have you got the gear on then? Have you got your sussies and cami-knickers on?"'

Sometimes he would walk round behind where Maureen was sitting and brazenly drop a hand over her shoulder and reach inside her blouse.

He would chance his luck, too, if one of the women offered to give him a lift anywhere. He'd immediately put a hand on their knee and they'd have to say, 'Now, cut that or you're not going.'

Anyone else, the women insist, would have got a right-hander and been shown the door, with a Geordie mouthful. But with Paul it was quite different: his antics and sug-gestiveness were so openly innocent that they never got upset or offended.

'How could we?' Margaret asks. 'He was always doing and saying the most outrageous, stupid things, it never entered our heads that he might be serious. Yes, he was stupid – very stupid. But not in a horrible way. He always treated us like mums. He'd drive you crackers, but you couldn't help liking him.'

Fortunately for Paul, these highly respectable, likeable ladies saw the funny side when he felt moved to take his trousers off in the office. He would like 'mooning' for them, too. Often, when a car was picking him up at the ground, he would toot the horn to attract the women's attention. When they looked out of the window they were confronted with the bare Gascoigne backside. He thought it was great fun.

'Other young lads used to take their trousers down and show us spots on their bottoms,' says Margaret. 'But Paul was the only one who mooned. He was a one-off.'

Paul is said to have demonstrated his gaucheness, if not lack of breeding, in the most alarming manner one day while he was staying at the home of his apprentice pal, Ian Bogie.

Looking at Ian's mother, sunbathing in a bikini in the garden, Paul allegedly opined, 'I'd like to give her one.'

It says much for Mr Bogie's reasonableness that he opted for a bucket of cold water to rebuke Paul for his rudeness – not a right-hander!

Whether Paul did have sex with lots of girls in those early years is open to question. Certainly he seemed keen to impress on the lottery ladies that he was getting his fair share.

Margaret says, 'He was always coming in and saying things like, "I had a right one last night," and telling us what he'd been up to. We were all very worried for him and told him to watch out or he'd have AIDS before he was twenty-one.'

Whenever Gazza did make the Newcastle side, his unique brand of humour, as much as his dazzling skill, caused a buzz among spectators, both home and away. By December, he had been named the North-East Young Player of the Month four times. And, a month later, after he had earned the Fiat Uno award yet again, former Newcastle favourite Jackie Milburn bubbled with excitement as he paid Gazza the ultimate tribute.

'I cannot remember a better player coming into the game in the last thirty years,' said Milburn, whose speed and shooting skills thrilled Geordie fans in the fifties. 'Young Gascoigne has the lot. I'll go and watch him anywhere – even in practice or five-a-side games.'

Milburn, who served on the Fiat Uno panel, chaired by England manager Bobby Robson, then predicted: 'I believe Gascoigne has it in him to take over from Bryan Robson as the eventual England captain.'

Milburn's judgement was sound. England Under-21 boss Dave Sexton had seen Gazza in a match at West Bromwich early in 1986 and had liked what he saw. He told Bobby Robson, and a week later the England manager watched Gazza in Newcastle's return match with Queens Park Rangers. He, too, was impressed.

For the boy who had learned to kick on the cobbled streets of a Gateshead backwater, the international scene was being set.

Although by late January Gazza had made only sixteen league appearances, other clubs were showing interest in him; and, while he and the rest of the team were enjoying a winter break in Bermuda, West Ham made a tentative approach. Newcastle told them their rising young star was not for sale.

On the field, Gazza was pleased with his progress, if a little disappointed that he had not turned on the style for Bobby Robson's England right-hand man, Don Howe, during Newcastle's 1–0 home win over Arsenal on 1 March. But he had now scored seven goals and seemed to be on target for the ten he had set himself after his QPR debut.

Off the field, Gazza had slipped back into his bad eating habits and his weight was worrying Willie McFaul and Colin Suggett. To force him to get the weight off, they introduced a system that would hit Paul where it hurt if he did not slim down – his pocket. They set a weight they felt he should be and said he would be fined £1 for every pound he was over it. Suggett would study the scales closely every Friday morning.

The thought of losing pounds in cash weighed heavily indeed on Paul's mind. He lost half a stone in four days and vowed, 'The days of fish and chips and fast food are over.'

Glenn Roeder, particularly, was concerned at Gazza's wayward lifestyle; like McFaul, he could see a glittering future for Gazza, but feared he could throw it all away. Roeder arranged for Gazza to meet Alistair Garvie, a tall, slim Scotsman, who was the club's assistant secretary. He was handling Chris Waddle's business affairs and Roeder thought he would be good for Gazza, too.

The meeting, Garvie remembers, took place in a working men's cafe in Whickham, a couple of miles from St James's. And he was not impressed with the casually dressed youngster Roeder insisted was going to be a big name.

'I hadn't seen the lad play,' says Garvie. 'I just trusted

Glenn's judgement. But my first impression of Gazza was that he was daft. It was the way he carried on and talked. He was hyperactive, never sitting still and always looking around. He couldn't seem to concentrate on anything.

'I certainly didn't see the potential in him from a commercial point of view, but I took a chance and signed a contract with him, agreeing to try my best to get him some publicity and, hopefully, some work.

'To be honest, he was a disaster area. I spent money trying to make things happen, but no one was interested. He was not well known enough, but, worse, he was hard to deal with, and most people who met him didn't like him because he was stupid and would mess around, doing daft things.'

It had been a mixed first season for Gazza. The St James's Park faithful admired his artistry and inventiveness, but they were frustrated, often angered, at the number of times he was caught in possession and by his slipshod defensive play. Being a young local lad, not known for his modest nature, he became a target for the terrace boo-boys who felt he needed bringing down a peg or two.

Not surprisingly, his confidence took a battering, and he admitted that at times he was so depressed he could not face the fans in the street, saying, 'All I want to do is get a football out and kick it against a brick wall to get rid of my frustration.'

Gazza also gave the first faint signs of possible financial unrest. Many people, he claimed, viewed him as a rich superstar wanting for nothing, when in fact his take-home pay from a basic £120 a week was just £85, without bonuses. His contract had a year to run and he was happy with that. But he added, somewhat guilelessly, 'If the boss wants to talk a new financial deal in the summer because he thinks I've earned it, then that's fine.'

He told people he was happy where he was and did not want to move to another club. According to Alistair Garvie, however, Gazza wanted to leave Newcastle almost from the moment he got into the first team.

'He wanted to go because the crowd and the people at the club were on his back,' says Garvie.

'Paul just wanted to get away. He's an emotional sort of kid and he'd spend hours on the phone to me, pouring his heart out, pleading with me to do something, as soon as *any* club showed an interest in him.

'He was fed up about always being skint. He never told me about his poor upbringing, but I'd heard his family were skint, too. He always said he wanted to make loads of money, but he always gave away a lot of what he earned or blew it in the betting shop.

'I had to explain that there was little we could do because he was under contract. He seemed to understand and, a day later, would say he was happy and wanted to stay. But when another club was reported to be interested in him, he'd be on the phone again, saying, "I want away." He was dissatisfied because he thought the people were difficult to get on with. But the truth is *he* was difficult to get on with. He looked to people to butter him up, then he'd take advantage of them. He used to drive me mad.

'And his general behaviour around town caused me many sleepless nights. I was forever wondering where he was and worrying about what he was up to. I was like a mother to him.'

If Garvie was concerned about Gazza's behaviour off the field, McFaul was far from happy with his conduct *on* it. True, he had banged in all but one of the ten goals he had promised, and, yet again, had been named the North-East Young Player of the Month. But his quick temper had repeatedly got him into trouble, and his playing season ended on a sour note on 13 April when he was sent off – and later fined by McFaul – for hitting Birmingham City's Robert Hopkins in Newcastle's 4–1 victory.

The fans, however, forgave Gazza his inconsistency and temper. Like Jackie Milburn, they knew a star when they saw one, and they voted Gazza the club's Most Exciting Player of the Year. The message from St James's Park was loud and very clear: love or hate Paul Gascoigne, it was impossible to ignore him.

The soccer-daft Gateshead kid's dream of entertaining the people of Newcastle with a football had become a reality at last.

9

The battle of the bulge continued throughout the close season, and when Paul reported back for pre-season training he had lost 11lb, earning a tribute from McFaul. 'Losing weight at a time when players traditionally put it on is a tremendous compliment to Gascoigne,' he said publicly. 'He's come back with a tremendous attitude, ready for what is a very important season.'

Unhappily that season got off to an appalling start for Paul before even a ball had been kicked in the league. He picked up a knee injury after just forty-five minutes in a warm-up tournament in the Isle of Man; while the rest of the Newcastle squad went to Ireland for friendlies against Coleraine and Linfield, Paul sailed back to England to see a specialist. He made the opening match, against Liverpool, but was brought off injured and missed the following week's 1–1 draw with Spurs. He returned against Luton and Sheffield Wednesday, then scored the only goal of the game against Wimbledon to give Newcastle their first win of the season. But the team was not playing well, and neither was Paul. He was relegated to substitute for the following game, at Norwich, and a few days later found himself in the reserves with other out-of-touch first-teamers.

Warnings that, after such a good debut season, he would not find life in the First Division so comfortable this time around were proving to be right. Wherever he played, Paul was a marked man, and given little time on the ball to

Joy: Paul (*third from right, bottom row*), aged 13, in the 'big team' – the Redheugh Boys Under-13s.

Fighting Weight: Paul lost £1 for every 1 lb he gained, but the scheme and coach Colin Suggett got him in trim.

The Big Break: Paul aged 18, when he signed as a pro for Newcastle.

Heroes: Football legend Jackie Milburn predicted that Paul would be an England star.

Up, Up and Away: Paul salutes the Newcastle home crowd after the third goal against Chelsea in 1988 and sets the transfer market buzzing.

Loving Son: (*above*) Paul cuddles his mum, Carol.
(*below*) Paul with his dad, John.

Gotcha!: Vinny Jones gets a vice-like grip on Paul to 'teach him a lesson' in their league clash in 1988.

Testing Time: Terry Venables keeps a close eye on Paul at one of his first Spurs training sessions in August 1988.

Gissa Kiss: Happy times with Bobby Robson, but behind the smiles Paul was fighting for his England chance.

(*Photograph* Ron Hewitt)

The Tears: Paul sobs after the heart-break of the West Germany defeat.

display his rich skills. This led to frustration and retaliation and, eventually, the inevitable yellow card. Paul's confidence began to sag. And the more the team played badly and lost, the less confidence Paul had to do the things he was good at, such as playing quick one-twos and making penetrating runs into the opposing penalty area.

He had been looking forward to the season so much, seeing it as his chance to continue to impress and, possibly, win an England Under-21 cap. Now, it was all going wrong.

John Pickering, who had been brought in as first-team coach, says, 'Working and tackling hard were not Gazza's strong points. He'd start off well, but then that side of his game would fade out. The only time he would chase back and tackle hard was when he lost his temper after making a bad pass. That's when he'd give away a foul and possibly be booked.

'David McCreery was a great ball-winner and grafter and he'd cover up when Gazza lost the ball or was slow getting back. If it hadn't been for him, Gazza's faults would have been harder on the team. To be fair, the lad appreciated the work Davy did because he knew that, without him, the weakness in his own game would show through more. On the other hand, Gazza could do things with the ball that Davy couldn't, so it was a good combination.

'Gazza was determined to do his own thing and he believed what he was doing was right. He did do things wrong, but there were certain aspects of his play – like his ability to turn a game – that made you say, "We'll abide with him and keep him," and hope the faults could be ironed out.

'Gazza's main fault at the start of that season was that he was determined to do his own thing. In training, when we were trying to get team work and pattern play organized, Gazza would fidget and not take any notice of what was being said. Yet he would then go and do exactly what you wanted – although not in the way you had told him.

'Before a match, he could never sit still. He was always on the go, always wanting to be doing something. It was very difficult giving him instructions, not because he might not be paying attention, but you wouldn't want to ruin his game. If you say too much to a player of such high ability it can knock the flair out of them, because they're concentrating too much on the instructions. You want them to work for the team, of course, but you don't want them to be the same as everyone else because that's not why they're there. They're there to bring that bit extra and get the crowd on the edge of their seats.

'He'd frustrate you by not listening and get himself in trouble in the game. But, just as you start rollocking him, he would suddenly get out if it and do something well. He gave you a hard time, but you'd always end up putting your arm round him afterwards because he just had that feeling for the game that made your anger go away. You could always see in Gazza's face that he took a pride in his performance and wanted to do well.'

Nowhere was Paul's nervous energy more apparent than in a hotel on the Friday night before a Saturday away match. Senior pros would be in bed by 10 p.m. at the latest after dinner, but it was too early for Paul; he couldn't just go to his room and lie on the bed – he wanted to be on the move all the time, doing something. He would always be larking about with the receptionists, and generally pushing his luck with his manager and coach as far as he could.

John Pickering says, 'At between 10.45 and 11 p.m. he'd still be around and would start talking to you about something totally meaningless, purely to side-track you so that he could stay up for another ten minutes or whatever. He wasn't doing anything bad – he was just a young lad pushing his luck. He was always the last to go to bed. But even then he wouldn't go to sleep. He'd keep his room-mate awake, either by chatting or watching television.'

Eventually, McFaul encouraged some of the senior pros, such as Roeder, Goddard and McCreery, to take Gazza under their wing and teach him the mature preparation for a game and to make sure he did not get into mischief. Gradually, Gazza began to understand and calmed down.

McFaul, as disheartened as anyone by Paul's performances at the start of that 1986–87 season, dropped him into the reserves again, complaining, 'He's trying to do too much on his own. The sooner he realizes he hasn't got the right to dominate a game the better.'

Paul was brought on as substitute in an away match against Aston Villa, and then given the chance to put everything right in front of his adoring, and patient, fans against Oxford on the Saturday before Guy Fawkes' Day.

Sadly, Paul's promise of a cracking display of fireworks fizzled out into a disappointing soaking-wet squib, and he played so badly he was substituted.

McFaul, who had decided to play Paul at the last minute, was furious that he was still trying to do too much on his own, hanging on to the ball too long and squandering good scoring chances. But the final straw came when, after an atrocious performance, when he did nothing right, he was caught in possession near his own area and almost presented Oxford with a goal. When he was called off, Paul trooped dejectedly to the dugout, booed by the fans who only the previous season had cheered him.

Later, he admitted it was the worst footballing experience of his life: the crowd had got on to him before, but this time they had frightened him and he could not handle it. His confidence, he said, went in the first fifteen minutes and never came back.

McFaul was frustrated by Paul's poor form, but not unduly surprised: he knew from experience that all youngsters hit bad spells in their early first-team days. He was not surprised, either, when another First Division club approached him about buying Paul and his pal from apprentice days, Paul Stephenson.

The club was Wimbledon. And while McFaul told the

London club's manager, Dave Bassett, that the boys were not for sale, he was quietly pleased about the inquiry: it might help put the sparkle back into his subdued youngsters. 'Every player has his price,' he told the local press with a look of deadly seriousness.

The quote could not inspire Paul's game at that moment, because a groin strain that had come on against Oxford had kept him out of action. But it generated more than a little financial interest. Every player has his price, McFaul had said; well, Paul wanted to get away at *any* price – even to unfashionable Wimbledon. He wanted to get away from the boo-boys on the terraces, and he wanted to solve his cash problems. Excitedly, he got on to agent Alistair Garvie and asked him to do what he could to pull off a deal. Garvie, however, quickly reminded Paul he had signed a three-year contract in August and a transfer was out of the question.

Paul was disappointed, and over the next few weeks his frustration got worse. After being brought on as a second-half substitute for a Full Members' Cup tie at Everton, early in December, he suffered another groin injury in a reserve team game the following night, and was out of action until after Christmas.

For such a hyperactive youngster who wanted only to play football, the lay-off was to prove not only irritating to Paul, but worrying for the club and McFaul in particular. Injuries such as groin strains need rest, but Paul was not the type to sit around doing nothing. Soon, his frustration turned to boredom and this, in turn, led to trouble.

'Everything was happening for the lad and he was finding it hard to cope,' says John Pickering. 'He needed to have a ball at his feet. He found it tough because he didn't know what to do with himself.

'His injury came at a bad time because he'd hit the spotlight. He started going astray. To many, he just got up to the pranks of a normal teenager, but he was so well known in Newcastle, any trouble he was involved in was highlighted.

'He wasn't an angel, by any means. He did stupid things – like tearing around recklessly in a car he'd just bought. It didn't seem to register with him that it was dangerous and that he just could not keep on doing it. The police would let him off with a warning, but someone always let it get back to the manager.'

An incident the police could not ignore happened one night just after 11 p.m. five days before Christmas at Broadway East, in the Gosforth area of Newcastle. Paul was driving a Renault 5 GTL, with his 22-year-old pal 'Fat' Jimmy Gardner in the passenger seat, and hit a man who stepped off the pavement at the junction with Strathmore Road. Paul stopped the car a few yards up the road for a few moments, then drove off.

Someone must have taken the car's registration number because Paul was later arrested and charged with various motoring offences, including failing to stop after an accident, failing to report it, and failing to display L-plates while being a learner driver. His unemployed friend, who also lived in Dunston, was charged with aiding and abetting Paul.

McFaul is quick to admit that, as Paul's enforced lay-off stretched into the New Year, the lad did cause problems. 'He was so impatient,' says McFaul. 'He took two or three times to pass his driving test, but took chances and drove anyway. I would tell him it had to stop, and that he was going to spoil everything for himself if he didn't mend his ways.

'Other players with the same injury responded to rest, but Paul didn't. He has a lot of nervous energy and he got involved in so many activities that I don't think he got enough rest. People in the North East latch on to good players and, at that time, everyone wanted to be with him and buy him a drink.'

In the first week of January, one month after that reserve team game against Everton, McFaul and the club's physiotherapist, Derek Wright, became so worried at Paul's lack of progress they arranged for him to have tests. But they still failed to find a solution and Paul was sent to a second specialist in groin injuries. Again, his X-rays were clear and Paul was ordered to have a further examination to explore the possibility of something being wrong with his lower stomach. But the tests did nothing to clear up the mystery and there seemed little Paul could do, except sit it out and let nature work a cure.

Being unable to train, he had had little to do with Colin Suggett. But now, with Paul's flair badly needed in a Newcastle side facing relegation, the demanding coach crossed the Tyne bridge into Gateshead and took Paul swimming at the public baths.

'He wasn't a good swimmer at first, but he became one,' says Suggett. 'It was either that or drown – because once I'd started the clock, he wasn't allowed to stop. I started him on twenty lengths, increased to twenty-five and, finally, to thirty. Those sessions increased his lung capacity and stamina, and took off a few pounds.

'Gazza pushed himself as usual and one day he helped another young player I felt needed swimming exercise. The lad did just four lengths and stopped, but Gazza got him going by challenging him to a race. With other lads, I may have been tempted to leave them to it. But I couldn't trust them. If I'd left, they'd have got out and had a lark about.'

By February, Paul was back in training and, despite having to have stitches in a leg wound, was in contention for a place in the squad for an FA Cup tie at Tottenham on 21 February. But, ten days before the game, bad luck struck again: he limped out of a full-scale practice match at Gateshead Stadium after twisting a knee on the artificial surface.

Fortunately, the twist was not as serious as it looked, and felt, at the time and Paul was fit enough to turn out for the reserves at Coventry just three days before the Spurs game. His long lay-off affected him, however, and he came off at half-time with a pulled thigh muscle. His dream of returning to first-team action in front of a capacity White Hart Lane crowd was over. Instead, the next morning, he was on Derek Wright's treatment table again.

If it was frustrating for Paul, it was maddening for McFaul. With Newcastle still struggling at the foot of the First Division, he badly wanted Paul fit again to boost a team whose confidence was now at rock-bottom.

Happily, the thigh injury seemed to clear within a couple of days and McFaul pencilled in Paul in the senior side for a crunch game against Wimbledon in the last week of February. But, unbelievably, Paul's injury jinx continued: he broke down in training with a strain higher up the same leg and was ruled out indefinitely.

The kid who just lived to play had not kicked a first-team ball for 120 agonizingly frustrating days. And now the chances of getting back in the side before the end of the season were decidedly slim. If Newcastle were going to avoid the drop into the Second Division, it seemed that they would have to do it without him.

And that pre-season dream of an England Under-21 cap – what a joke! How could Dave Sexton even think about picking a player who had spent most of his time on the treatment table or in the swimming baths.

To a large extent, Paul brought his troubles on himself. As John Pickering says, 'He wanted to play so badly he came back two or three times before he was fit, because he thought he could get away with it. But he only aggravated his injuries and they set him back even further. That, in turn, led to him putting on weight and he quickly got out of condition.'

Newcastle's plight became more desperate when an injury against Manchester United ruled striker Peter Beardsley out for the rest of the season.

And then, suddenly, Paul's own problems cleared. On 11 March, Willie McFaul played him in a reserve team game against Aston Villa at St James's Park, praying his performance would be good enough to justify picking him for the following week's crucial first-team match against Manchester City.

It was.

After more than four months of being a spectator, the clown prince was ready to take centre-stage in the thrilling drama of the Magpies' flight from the depths to Division One safety. Over the next few weeks, wins over Manchester City, Arsenal and Norwich and a gritty draw away to West Ham guaranteed First Division football at St James's Park the following season, and left McFaul's Irish eyes smiling with relief.

Today, he is full of praise for Gazza.

'He did one helluva job,' he says. 'We had missed him, and you didn't expect to miss someone so young. We were struggling badly, particularly with Beardsley out, but Paul came back and made a big difference.

'We needed a result against Arsenal and we got it. We knew we were better than the results we'd been getting. Paul was an influence, and instrumental in our 1–0 win. He wasn't the be-all and end-all; he didn't do it on his own. But the other players respected his ability and his enthusiasm and, there's no doubt, it made a difference to them. He took over from Beardsley and did the job.

'I noticed a change in him. Being out of the game for so long made him appreciate it more. He was still frustrating to play with at times, but the other lads appreciated his talent and not one would ever dream of saying he couldn't play.'

The players' view of that talent is, perhaps, best summed up by Paul Stephenson. 'You couldn't put your finger on one thing he would do – it was a number of things. He would do things on the ball that none of the other older, more experienced, players would even think of trying. He was that cocky and confident in his ability that he never worried about anything and just got on with the games.'

It was a talent, however, that McFaul thought Paul was

going to waste during those dark winter months when those niggling injuries forced him off the field and into trouble.

'There was a time then when I feared he couldn't handle it and was going to disappear,' says McFaul. 'I thought he had lost it and said to myself, "What a waste of talent." It was impossible for myself or his coaches to be with him twenty-four hours a day, and he was getting into so many little scrapes that I put a question mark over him.

'Glenn Roeder was always looking out for Paul and would tell me certain things about him that I didn't know. Glenn thought it was for Paul's own good, and he was right. He would come into my office with Paul and speak for him when I had a go and demanded to know what the hell he was doing.

'I warned him regularly that he was going to disappear up his own backside if he didn't mend his ways. He would sit there and listen and appear to be taking it all in, but I was never really sure if I was getting through to him or not.

'There were times when I was worried that everyone seemed to be getting at him, but I always knew that, in the long run, it would be for his own good. He was lucky he was brought up in a crowd of players who cared; who, like me, didn't want to see that outstanding talent wasted. If he hadn't been watched, he could easily have gone the other way.

'He used to excite me in training. His vision was quite extraordinary for someone so young and relatively inexperienced. I don't think many managers would have taken a chance with him. But I was prepared to because of the incredible belief Paul had in his own ability and because he could give the Geordie public something to shout about. They love a player who can wiggle his bum a bit, and they'd been starved of entertainment for so long.

'Paul wanted to be the best. He didn't actually come out and say it, just gave you that impression because he was more determined than most, regarding his ability. He wanted to produce that ability on centre-stage. And if he was entertaining the crowds I loved it.

'I gave him the licence to do certain things and, I have to be honest, some didn't please me. He was the type of player who had that way that made you love them and then, the next minute, have you tearing your hair out. He could lose you a match by doing silly things, but he got better and better and revelled in the big occasions. I was prepared to give young people a break generally, but it pleased me more than anything else that I gave Paul his chance.'

Paul had played just twelve first-team games, but his impact on the fans had been so great, particularly in the relegation battle, that Newcastle supporters named him Most Exciting Player of the Year for the second successive year.

And then, on 7 May, the end to what had been a frustrating season was made even happier for Paul when Willie McFaul called him into his office.

'Dave Sexton just telephoned. He wants you for his England Under-21 squad.'

10

Paul did two things when that nerve-wracking season ended: he asked Alistair Garvie to look into the possibility of a move to Sheffield Wednesday, the latest club to approach Willie McFaul about him; and then he asked McFaul for two or three days off before joining the England Under-21 squad in London. Paul said he was exhausted and, apart from anything else, wanted to go fishing.

The answer was a resounding No on both counts. Garvie was happy to inquire about the Yorkshire club's interest, but the manager had made it clear to Wednesday boss Howard Wilkinson that Paul was definitely not for sale. As for going fishing, Paul could forget that, too: the only bait he should be interested in right now, said McFaul, was a full England cap – and the Under-21 tournament in Toulon was a big step towards getting one. So, instead of starting a summer break, Paul was told to report to Benwell for training to keep himself in shape.

'I want you to be sharp for Toulon, so that you can do yourself justice,' said McFaul.

Paul certainly did that. In the first match, against Morocco, he scored the first goal with a typically inventive free-kick and laid on the second in England's 2–0 win, then shone in a goalless draw with Russia. Sadly, Paul had to miss the showdown with France because of 'flu, but he then scored the deciding spot-kick in a penalty shoot-out against Portugal and generally had a good tournament.

The team's trainer, Mike Kelly, remembers Paul for his hyperactive behaviour not only on the pitch but off it, too. 'In the practice games before the tournament he was a bit haywire and we had to try to keep him on a leash,' says Mike. 'He always wanted to be in the thick of things and would go all over the field, trying to do everyone's job.

'He has a bright mind and would listen if he was directly involved in training. But when he wasn't, he found it difficult to concentrate and would find something to do, like juggling a ball or kicking it at someone. He always wanted to be playing with the ball.

'At the airport or hotel reception – in fact, any public place – Paul was always the first to get fidgety. He'd get a ball out of one of the bags or he'd start knocking up with an orange – anything he could think of. He loved to look for challenges – like throwing things in a bin from a long distance, or throwing peanuts into someone else's glass. He's got a good eye for those sort of things.

'As trainer, I didn't spend much time in his company. He spent a lot of time in his hotel room, or someone else's, getting up to pranks and generally larking around out of my sight.

'He was always shouting. If his hotel room was, say, six floors up, he'd always find it necessary to have a conversation with someone beside the pool. That sort of behaviour can be disruptive and give the England team a bad image, so, if he was out of order, I'd put a stop to it. I'd never have to make a big deal: one "Oi!" and a look would be enough. Mind you, ten minutes later, he'd be up to something else!

'He's a happy-go-lucky extrovert, who wants to have fun every minute of the day. With the Under-21s, he was at his best – or worst, whichever way you want to look at it – when he had an audience and felt he could be a nuisance.

'He was very popular and the lads found him funny, but if you're in his company all the time, he wears you down and, finally, you've got to get away for a bit of peace.

'As far as his game was concerned, we all knew he had talent. But Dave Sexton knew there were faults in his game – like his poor defensive play – and when he talked to Bobby Robson or myself, we all took the view, "The kid's got the talent – what can we do to the team to help him?"'

Tony Dorigo, then of Aston Villa, was the Under-21 captain for the tournament. He admits that trying to look after Paul on the pitch was 'slightly impossible'.

'It was hard to fit him into the framework of the team, because he has a mind of his own,' says Tony. 'He would be told what position he was in, and what to do and what not to do, but, once on the pitch, he would do his own thing. Yet, no matter where he was, he would end up doing something brilliant. After he's scored a great goal, you couldn't go up to him and say, "Hey, you were out of position – you should be back here."

'If you did shout at him, he'd listen, but it didn't really sink in. He does what he wants to. Dave Sexton talked to him about his game a lot and it worried Paul that Dave wasn't happy about some of it. Despite the impression he gives, Paul, takes his football very seriously indeed – it's everything to him and he never seems to be bored with playing.

'In a tournament in Aberdeen, after Toulon, we were warming up and the weather was atrocious. The wind was howling and rain was pouring down and all the lads were wrapped up in their tracksuits, not too keen to get going. But Paul was out there in his shorts, whacking balls around as though it was a perfect day for a game. He loves the game. He goes at it full pelt all the time and never tires.

'We were in Toulon for about ten days and, naturally, we had a lot of free time. One day all the lads were sunbathing on the roof of the hotel and, as usual, Paul got a bit bored. He started mixing a drink in a long glass, then went round all the players in turn, trying to persuade each one to drink it.

'He'd say, "G'on, I'll give you a tenner." Everyone took a sniff and said, "No way," but when it was Steve Sedgeley's turn, he said, "I'll do it – but only if you make it a hundred quid."

'Paul couldn't believe it. He was really excited. "Hang on a sec'," he said. "I'll get the other lads to chip in."

'We all agreed to make up the money, then Paul started adding aftershave, sun lotion and other things to his cocktail to make it worth the extra money.

'Steve took one sip and was almost sick. He couldn't take any more. That sort of thing was typical of Paul – he had to be up to something and have everyone laughing and mucking around.'

It was on that Toulon trip that Tony discovered, to his surprise, that Paul was a keen fisherman.

'A couple of the lads had brought some girlie magazines, which were left in a loo at the end of a corridor in the hotel,' says Tony.

'Paul was in there for about twenty minutes one day and I had to tell him to hurry up because I needed to use the toilet.

'I assumed he was engrossed looking at one of the girlie magazines, but when I went in I found myself looking at a picture of a 12 lb trout in an angling magazine!'

Certainly Dave Sexton thought England had landed a good catch with Paul on that tour.

As Robson says today: 'We had been looking at Gascoigne for over a year after Newcastle recommended him. I sent Dave Sexton to look at him a couple of times and it was on his recommendation we picked him for the Toulon tournament. Dave came home saying there were a lot of things wrong with Gascoigne's game, but many more that were good. He had a great football brain and a lot of talent and had been one of our best players. He was overweight and a bit stupid, but a good lad, with a bubbly personality, and easy to handle.'

Paul celebrated with his father and a handful of friends from Dunston who had flown to France, at Paul's expense, for the tournament.

He returned home, treasuring his England shirt. He had sampled international football, and it tasted sweet.

Certainly McFaul must take some credit for that promising debut. Peter Kirkley, who was sent to Toulon to monitor the games, said, 'Paul told me after the first training session that he felt he would do well, because he was so much fitter than the other lads. He was able to make surging sixty- and seventy-yard runs into the opposing penalty areas and was generally in peak condition.

'It was the France game that made people realize how well he'd played. England were lost without him and went down 2–0, costing them a place in the final.'

Paul returned to Newcastle in mid June with newspaper headlines singing his praises. But they hit a sour note only one week later when the local hero went to court to face the music over his motoring misdemeanour six months before. On the afternoon of 23 June, Paul and his friend Jimmy Gardner went before Newcastle magistrates and admitted all the charges made against them after the accident in Gosforth just before Christmas.

Paul was fined £150 for failing to stop after the accident, £100 for failing to report it, and £10 for not displaying L-plates. Gardner was fined £10 for aiding and abetting Paul when he failed to stop and report the accident.

Paul had little time to dwell on the fact that he now had a bad driving record before he had even passed his test. For within days he was excited to hear that Manchester United wanted to buy him. The news surprised Paul because United manager, Alex Ferguson, had publicly criticized his aggression when the two sides met at St James's Park in 1986. Nevertheless, Paul saw a move as attractive financially and immediately got on the phone to Alistair Garvie, urging him to try to push things along. A move was out of the question, particularly since Peter Beardsley was on his way to Liverpool, but United's interest did put Paul in a better bargaining position over an extension of the three-year contract he had signed a year before.

Anxious not to lose Paul in the same way as he had lost Chris Waddle and Beardsley, McFaul made a verbal offer, tying Paul to Newcastle until 1992. As the season began and he went to White Hart Lane for his fiftieth League appearance, Paul turned the offer down. He had fulfilled his dream of playing in the famous Magpie shirt, but the experience had not proved so rewarding that he wanted to wear it for another five years, despite the summer signing of a brilliant Brazilian whose dazzling skills might help Paul turn Newcastle into a powerful First Division force. Mirandinha watched Paul crown a glorious opening month with a spectacular show in the 1–0 defeat against Notts Forest. 'He's one of the best players I've seen. With his pace and dribbling skill, he's like a Brazilian.' And he predicted that Paul would become a 'very important' player for England.

Willie McFaul, though, was not impressed with Paul for losing the ball and giving away Forest's winning goal, and it led to a stiff after-match retort from Paul. He said he might as well go home at three o'clock if he was expected just to boot the ball away.

Thankfully, the Forest lapse did nothing to harm Paul's international chances and he was delighted, the next day, to be named in the Under-21 side to play West Germany in Ludenscheid the following week. Bobby Robson gave him an extra boost by saying, 'I've been greatly impressed when I've seen Gascoigne play for Newcastle, and Dave Sexton has given me a good report.'

One wonders if both men would have been so impressed had they known that Paul was carrying a knee injury he had picked up in the Forest game. He had kept it secret from his Newcastle boss and colleagues because he didn't want to pull out of the game. Now he hid it from Sexton, because he did not want to miss the chance of playing for his country.

It was an understandable, but professionally unacceptable character flaw, and it backfired on Paul in West Germany. He was unable to sprint or close players down quickly enough and took a couple of knocks. The longer the game went on, the angrier he got with himself and, inevitably, the worse he played. By half-time, manager Dave Sexton had seen enough and substituted him.

'He was all over the shop that night and, in my eyes, had lost control of himself and his game,' Sexton remembers. 'He was throwing himself into tackles far too physically and was always arguing with the ref. He was running around like a headless chicken.

'He was getting more and more uptight and his game was terrible. He was wild and would shout at the ref over the slightest decision. As far as I was concerned he was not behaving or playing the way an international player should. Being part of the Under-21s is all about learning how to control yourself. I would always tell the players that if you have not got the discipline, you've got nothing.

'It is so much easier to get booked and sent off in international football, and it was my job to watch them and teach them how to be an England player. All the players in my team knew that if they got booked they had an 80 per cent chance of coming off. I'm strict.

'Paul had all the talent, but was undisciplined. During the Germany game he was frantic and temperamental. I don't know for sure why he was so out of control, but I felt he was over-excited and was doing silly things.

'He was very aggressive, but not in a way that helped, because he wasn't playing well. He got frustrated, too, and his game became a mess. He wasn't playing a true midfield role.

'I had warned them all before the game that if they couldn't play in control of themselves then they would be off. So, as I watched Paul steadily get more out of line, I decided to give him a shock and teach him a lesson.

'At half-time, he was sitting down with the rest of them listening to me, and I told him straight: "You're coming off, Paul." I didn't have to explain my decision or go into detail.

'Paul was as good as gold, not cheeky or flippant. He just accepted my decision. There wasn't a row or any back-chat. He knew he wasn't playing well and had been sailing close to the wind. I'm sure he didn't like my decision, but he didn't show it, and sat with me on the bench for the second half. He was his normal self, shouting encouragement at the lads all through the rest of the game.

'A shock like that can do a player a lot of good if he has got the sense to realize his mistake. Thankfully, Paul has eventually taken it all in.

'When we got back to the hotel after the game, I pulled him aside for a private chat. I sat him down and talked to him quietly about what had gone wrong and what I was looking for from him. I told him I thought he had lost control of himself and his game. I said I didn't like the way he was behaving, I thought his tackles were reckless and would get him booked, and I told him never to talk back to referees.

'I didn't shout at him. I wanted him to learn from what I said, not get his back up. I was talking to a talented footballer whose talent I respected, and I was trying to help, not knock him – just trying to realize his potential.

'It is very easy for a shrewd opponent to get a player booked, then wind him again so he gets sent off. I had to drum it into Paul that he mustn't fall into that trap. He is temperamental and gets over-enthusiastic. Enthusiasm is a wonderful gift and I told him I liked that and never wanted it to go. But I told him it had to be channelled in the right way: positively and productively – not into wild play and rows with the ref. I told him there is no room in international football for arguing with referees.

'I also told him that I expected him to be the engine room in midfield. I needed him to be there, winning the ball and passing it, to open things up for the team. I didn't want him trying to impress everyone by going on long, dribbling runs all the time. He would tire himself out and not be able to get back where he should be on the field. I emphasized that he should do his midfield job first and his individual stuff later. I said I loved to see him wiggle and do his tricks, but he had to learn to be economical or he would wear himself out and be no good to the team.'

Paul, always a respectful and receptive lad with Sexton, listened carefully, taking in what his vastly experienced manager was telling him. He did not argue any point, or grumble that he was being singled out for specific criticism. He just took it on the chin, seeming to understand and appreciate that it was all for his own good.

That quiet, but stiff, talking-to was arguably the most significant warning Paul had been given since Jack Charlton's no-nonsense ultimatum three years before.

And it was one that Paul, astonishingly, would appear to have ignored, causing Sexton to despair and wonder if the boy would ever have the maturity to become a full England player.

Paul owned up to the injury when he returned to Newcastle and was immediately sent to a specialist in Jesmond. His fears of cartilage trouble proved unfounded, but he ended up back on Derek Wright's treatment table with lots of rest to follow. Once again, Paul's boundless enthusiasm for kicking a ball had, ironically, put him out of action again.

His absence was bad news for Newcastle. He was developing into an all-round player, with strength to match his skill, and his influence on the team's performance was incredible.

As Glenn Roeder put it, 'It may well be wrong for a First Division club to rely on someone so young to be playmaker, but that's the way it is. Paul had a bad time in our last home game because he was carrying that knee injury, and, consequently, we didn't play.'

With typical positive thinking, Paul accepted the Newcastle Chronicle/Hennessy Cognac Player of the Month for August award and vowed, 'I was upset at what happened in Germany and hope I've learned my lesson. I will come back fitter and stronger.'

And, then, off he went to Cragside Park, Rothbury, with his fishing pal, Stan Nixon, hoping to repeat the success they had had recently when they landed a 5½ lb rainbow trout.

Paul and Mirandinha hit it off from the moment the Newcastle team stood in a line to welcome the Brazilian at the Benwell training ground. Joker Paul shook hands with him at one end of the line, then quickly darted to the other to shake hands again. Although Mirandinha was bemused at the time, he saw the joke and the two became good off-the-field buddies. When Mirandinha had settled in at Bedlington with his family, he mentioned to Paul that his two sons – Diego, aged six, and Ernandes, four – wanted a dog. Paul promptly presented him with a ten-week-old springer spaniel, which Mirandinha, equally promptly, named 'Gazza'.

To return the compliment, Paul promised to call his goldfish 'Mirandinha'.

The Brazilian's English was coming along fine, Paul told

a local reporter: Mira's three main words, he said, were 'Gazza', 'flipping' and 'freezing'. What Paul chose not to reveal was that he taught Mirandinha three words before those and they made up a naughty phrase not to be found in any Oxford dictionary!

The two players seemed to appreciate and enjoy each other's skill, and it was not uncommon, as Paul got back to first-team fitness, for them to practise clever free-kicks together after training. Paul was particularly good at bending the ball round a life-size five-man 'wall' made out of tin, and he would help and encourage Mirandinha for anything up to an hour while other players were getting changed to go home. He had been out of league action for nearly a month and it was good to be kicking a ball again.

Although he was watching his weight closely now, temptation for chocolate was always round the corner and, on one occasion during that lay-off, he succumbed – to his cost. If no one was around, Paul would sneak into Willie McFaul's office and make calls to girls on the sexy phone-lines; according to groundsman David Orchard he would chat away for half an hour or so, purely for a laugh. One day, he was about to dial one of the advertised numbers when he saw a half-eaten Kit-Kat bar on the manager's desk. Without thinking, he picked it up and started munching away. He had nearly finished when an apprentice came in and told Paul that someone had put the chocolate on McFaul's desk because they had found a maggot in it.

Horrified, Paul raced out of the office on to the grass, coughing and spluttering, trying his best to bring up the offending grub.

When Paul returned to the first team against Chelsea in September, he had got down to what he considered his 'fighting weight' – 11 st 11 lb – but that didn't stop the Stamford Bridge fans taunting him with shouts of 'Fatty'. Paul, delighted to be back in action, showed them his class, then, at the final whistle, he showed them his tummy – in a cheeky gesture that the wags in the 'Shed' loved.

His impish sense of humour and off-the-wall antics made him a favourite on the terraces when things were going well. But they were not appreciated when Newcastle were losing. Peter Kirkley had always seen Paul as nothing more than a great entertainer whom the crowd would love, not for himself but for what he could do with a ball, no matter what the score was. But it had not turned out that way: Paul was a vital cog in the Newcastle wheel and when he failed to function – or functioned badly – the wheel stopped turning. In the midweek Littlewoods Cup tie against Blackpool a few days later, for instance, a disastrous back pass by Paul let in former team-mate Tony Cunningham, and Newcastle could not get back into the game. Paul's artistry earned a few cheers that night, but Newcastle travelled home a goal behind on the first leg.

Embarrassed, as well as angry, at his lapse, Paul promised the fans a goal in the second leg at St James's Park. And he kept that promise, hitting the winner near the end after Newcastle had levelled the score. It was his first goal of the season and he celebrated it with all the pizzazz and uninhibited joy he showed when he hit the net as a schoolboy.

It was chilly that October night but the welcome that goal got on the terraces was warm, and Paul sank to his knees then did a jig of delight.

Hardly had his euphoria calmed down than fate dumped Paul on his backside again. Dave Sexton, far from happy with that ill-disciplined first-half in West Germany, left him out of the side for the Turkey game at Sheffield.

Paul was hurt but admitted the wound to his pride was self-inflicted. He understood that players had to be judged by international standards and, as his last England game was poor, it had, understandably, counted against him.

And Paul agreed with Mirandinha, who reminded him he had only just started and had not made it yet. Paul admitted there was a lot he had to learn about the game, and the lesson he had to learn now was not to waste his next break with the Under-21s – if he was lucky enough to get one.

He *was* lucky enough. Sexton picked him for the game against Yugoslavia on 10 November. But Paul went into the match with a stern warning from club manager Willie McFaul following Newcastle's exit from the Littlewoods Cup. Paul missed three clear chances at Wimbledon and McFaul said, 'In his first season, he scored nine goals from midfield. He should now be aiming for fifteen – and that's the bottom line. His talent is tremendous and exciting, but he has got to change to fulfil his potential and go all the way. He has got to grow up – and learn to finish off his good work.'

It was Paul's poor finishing that made certain Newcastle fans get on his back, prompting former manager Jack Charlton to make a passionate plea to them to lay off.

'Paul is the best player Newcastle have got,' he said, 'and everything revolves around him.'

And Charlton added, prophetically, 'If he were to go elsewhere he would be a really big star, and it's about time Newcastle supporters realized this.'

The writing seemed to be on the wall, even then. Newcastle soccer fans, while passionate and fervent, were fickle: they wanted Paul to display his rich repertoire, but were merciless in their criticism when it didn't come off; they cheered him when he scored seemingly unbelievable goals, but jeered when he missed relatively easy ones. They wanted to admire him as a thoroughbred, but howled in despair when he didn't do the donkey work. Whatever Paul did, he could never do it well enough, couldn't win. As the season reached the half-way mark, he was fed up with it.

And then, with exquisite timing, Bobby Robson travelled to the North East to see his mum and dad and watch a football match. The game he chose would convince him that Paul would be going to the World Cup in 1990.

11

The match was Newcastle's FA Cup fourth-round tie against Swindon at St James's Park, later to hit the headlines in the Lou Macari betting scandal. Paul scored two goals in Newcastle's 5–0 victory and generally had a good game, ripping the Swindon defence to pieces whenever he got the ball. But it was not just his overall performance that impressed Bobby that blustery January afternoon; it was the supreme confidence that went with everything he did, or tried. Paul was a kid playing with men, but he had the air of someone in their mid twenties who had been around. And it had an effect on Bobby, watching from the directors' box. He knew Paul, of course, because of his Under-21 appearances, and it made Bobby's mind flash back to what Jackie Milburn had told him all those years before. What was it Jackie had said? 'We've got a lad coming through in the juniors, Bob – he's going to be great.' Well, he's certainly come on a lot, Bobby thought, as Paul began to enjoy the easy victory.

Today, Bobby remembers the game well. 'The lad's overall game was very good,' he says. 'I thought he had a lot of talent, but it was clear it needed to be harnessed, and one would have to build a team to suit *him*. He played in a loose midfield role that day – the free man, with two eager beavers around him doing all the tracking, marking and winning the ball. He had no strong defensive duties; he was in-between and would just wait to be given the ball to play. It suited him because he was a bit carefree and undisciplined.

'He was clever on the ball and could dribble past people. He had a good eye for a pass and always looked dangerous. But when an attack broke down, he just kind of sauntered back into midfield without any specific defensive role, and was on hand to pick up the ball again when his mates had won it back.

'What he did with the ball was always skilful and positive, but he was a bit careless at times and slightly obsessed with playing that one extra clever pass. He was always looking to take the mickey out of a situation.

'He scored twice – once with a penalty, which he bashed into the net so cheekily, arrogantly, if you like. He played that cheeky, cocky way throughout the match and I remember it struck me that he was playing with the confidence of someone much older. He was one of those kids who, if he made a mistake or did something stupid, never seemed upset; never seemed worried or anxious when things he's trying aren't coming off.'

In the visitors' lounge after the game, Bobby asked Willie McFaul about Paul. It was obvious the manager thought the world of him.

'What you've seen today is him,' McFaul said simply. 'He can open up a defence and score a goal, but he tends to play only when he's got the ball. He's very clever and can be the difference between winning and losing. But you can't rely on him. Other people have to work for him when we haven't got the ball.'

McFaul, the former England manager remembers, said he was trying to discipline Paul to mature as a player and do things in a game for the benefit of the team, not just himself.

'While we were talking I noticed Paul come into the lounge,' says Bobby. 'I could see him, out of the corner of my eye, staring at me, maybe in awe, because I was the England manager and he was just a young kid not long in the Newcastle first team. He didn't come up to me, just stayed chatting with his friends while I talked to Willie in the directors' area.

'I was fully aware of who he was and what he'd done on the field that day. And I knew, in my heart, that we could

124

not possibly leave him out of the squad for Italy. He may not make the starting line-up, but he was one of those exciting players who we could stick on in the last half hour if we were losing 1–0 in a tough match, to get a goal for us, or make one. We would have to cater for him.'

Private though those thoughts were at that time, Bobby did give a broad public hint of Paul's World Cup hopes, possibly because of talk in the North East that the lad would have to leave Newcastle to win a full cap.

Advising Paul to stay and help bring successful football back to the area, Bobby said, 'It doesn't matter where you play, it matters that you're the best in your position. If you are, you'll be selected. There's no question of a North–South divide.'

Then, referring to Paul as 'a little gem', he urged: 'Forget the European Championships this summer and set your sights on the World Cup in 1990.'

Bobby admitted he had not closed the door on Paul going to the European Championships; but he stressed that the boy would have to 'play out of his skin every match until the end of the season'.

McFaul himself remembers telling Bobby about Paul's temperament, as much as his footballing ability; that he was still as hot-headed as ever and would do silly things in a game that would get him sent off.

'Basically, I said that I was not going to stand in the lad's way, but, in my opinion, he wasn't ready for England – and England wasn't ready for him. I told him the same as I told Dave Sexton when he rang for progress reports: the talent is there and he can do all sorts of marvellous things – but he'll drive you round the bend at times!'

The week after their FA Cup win, Newcastle went to Wimbledon for a League match. Paul went through a traumatic experience on the pitch that silenced his good-humoured banter and shattered his confidence for several weeks afterwards. It was an experience that shocked even the most seasoned pros in the Newcastle side.

When Newcastle had played Wimbledon in the Little-woods Cup the previous October, only to lose in injury time, Paul had had a brilliant game. True, he had missed those three good scoring chances, but his running on and off the ball had been a joy to watch, and he had controlled the midfield majestically.

Wimbledon's manager, Bobby Gould, and coach, Don Howe, had just the player to make sure he did not do the same in the league encounter. He was an uncompromising footballer with a fraction of Paul's ability and skill, but one hundred times the aggression. His name was Vinny Jones. And what he put Paul through at the Plough Lane ground on the afternoon of 6 February, became a talking point of soccer for the rest of the season.

From the first whistle, Jones was not interested in the ball, only where Paul was. Throughout a goalless first half, the Wimbledon 'hard' man tracked Paul wherever he ran or walked on the pitch, intimidating him in forty-five minutes of chilling adversity, bordering on hate. Jones shouted and swore at Paul incessantly. He sneered and belittled him. He spat at him in the face when the referee wasn't looking.

When he went to take a throw-in or corner, he would glare at Paul like a gangster in a B-movie and hiss menac-ingly, 'Don't move, Fat Boy – I'll be back.' On other occasions, he turned his back on the ball and stood a few inches from Paul, 'eyeballing' him fearsomely, boxing-ring fashion.

And then, in a moment fortuitously captured by a national newspaper photographer, Jones performed the act that incensed the Newcastle dugout, terrified Paul, and disgusted the nation.

Standing a few inches in front of Paul, waiting for a free-kick to be taken, Jones slyly put a hand behind him and clutched Paul's testicles through his shorts.

If the close attention Jones had given him throughout that first-half had intimidated Paul, that gesture squeezed

126

the last ounce of confidence from him, and he walked to the dressing room at half-time dejected, worried and apprehensive.

Coach John Pickering remembers the day well. He says: 'Paul was normally noisy at half-time, shouting at teammates if things were going badly, or bubbling with good-humour if they were going well. But at Wimbledon that day, he was quiet and subdued: his head was down and we couldn't console him. He knew what was in store for him in the second half and he didn't like it or know how to cope. He was dumbfounded by the treatment he'd received; it went against all his beliefs about the game.

'We all tried to comfort him and get him going, but, because we'd never come across such a situation before, none of us were sure how to handle it. All I could think of saying was, "Don't worry about it – it's a one-off situation and you won't get anything like that again." I told him he had so much ability he could overcome anything the likes of Vinny Jones chose to throw at him. But it was no good. Jones had set out to intimidate and dominate Paul and had succeeded. Paul didn't know what to do and neither did we.

'We decided to play him in a different position, out of midfield. It meant sacrificing his playmaking skills, but he wasn't being allowed to display them anyway, and it would get Jones out of the game as well, enabling us still to play through the middle and keep some shape. But, even in those extreme circumstances, it was hard to keep Paul out of the middle.'

Newcastle battled out a grim 0–0 draw and the team could not wait to get away from South London. It had been a most disquieting afternoon.

Pickering says he had never seen Paul so upset. 'He didn't say one word – he didn't even swear and shout about what had gone on – just sat in the dressing room, staring into space, his eyes all red from rubbing away the tears. He was crying out of shock and frustration that

Vinny had got the better of him. Not one of us in the dressing room had seen anyone treated so badly on a football pitch and we were sickened by it.

'Paul was usually one of the first to get in and out of the bath and get dressed, but that day he took a long time to get his football gear off. He was genuinely in a deep state of shock. Anything anybody said to him to try to buck him up wouldn't sink in. That's what made us realize just how bad the experience had been, and how much it had upset him. He started to liven up a bit on the bus to King's Cross station, but he wasn't the same Paul we knew and liked all the way home on the train. We were frightened other teams would pick up on that extraordinarily tight man-marking.

'One can't condemn Vinny Jones for doing what he did, although I am surprised the ref didn't speak to him about the way he was playing. I suppose you could say Jones did well on the day when you consider he hasn't got a third of Paul's talent – and that's being kind.'

Speaking today for the first time in detail about that day, Vinny Jones says: 'I didn't play in the first game, but I heard what a great game Gascoigne had had. When we reported for training on the Thursday before the return game, Bobby Gould and Don Howe told me they wanted me to mark him out of the game and we began a first-team versus the reserves match, with me marking someone in the Gascoigne role.

'It didn't work that day because I didn't really know what was expected, and Bobby and Don got uptight. They wanted me to really do the job there and then, but I couldn't get psyched up enough to put the pressure on.

'Half-way through the session, Don stopped the game and said, "Look, Vinny, if you can't do the job, or you don't want to do it, we'll play someone else." He gave me a lot of stick and that fired me up and I tried harder for the rest of the game. It still wasn't working completely though.

'After training, Don and I had a cup of tea together and

he explained about man-to-man marking. It meant shadowing Gascoigne for ninety minutes, not letting him have any access to the play.

'It had all been in the papers about Gazza leaving Newcastle and how he was worth £2 million and, during the warm up, photographers were running all round him and I thought: What a fat so and so! Who does he think he is? He was bubbly and looked like he was a bit of a character and a laugh. He didn't know who I was, or anyone on the Wimbledon side, but he didn't seem too bothered. He thought the whole day was about him and nobody else. There were ninety minutes to be played and he was prancing around like he was man of the match already. So I thought I would give him a rude awakening.

'All our lads had told me how good he was and how he'd tear us apart if we gave him an inch. I had to mark him the best I could and they would take care of the rest of the game. I told them I wouldn't let them down – and didn't. The game became ten against ten on that day, with Gazza and me having our own separate game.

'I set out to win the day and I wasn't going to stop at anything to do it. You have to do what you can, as long as it's not too far out of the game – I don't think referees see half of what goes on off the ball and the ref didn't that day either.

'I stuck with Gazza right from the first whistle and I was so close he started taking the mickey. "Is that all you can do, follow people around?" he said. I said, "Well, that's what I'm getting paid for today, son, so you'll have to put up with it."

'Then, I'd say, "If you're so good, and are meant to be the business, why are you so fat?" And he said, "I pay more in tax than you get wages." It was just banter. When I went to take a throw-in and said, "Don't go away, Fat Boy, I'll be back," he shook his head as if he thought I had a screw loose.

'Then Newcastle got a free-kick near the half-way line. I

was marking Gascoigne on the edge of the box and got in front of him. As the kick was about to be taken, he whispered something. I can't remember what, but it was probably something cheeky. I just grabbed out behind me and got hold of his nuts. I just squeezed to teach him a lesson for being so mouthy. It wasn't planned – it was just a split-second reaction. He yelled in pain and I let go and carried on playing.

'I had been told to mark him tightly and I went about it in such a way that he never touched the ball, but I touched *his* balls! Gazza was giving as good as he was getting with the verbals, and I honestly don't think I went over the top.

'He came out for the second half a different person. He had shut right up and wasn't giving me any lip any more. He went so quiet I didn't really have to stop him getting the ball – he didn't want it. That was it then – I knew I had done the job.

'Towards the end, he started taking me on a merry-go-round. He would run the opposite way to the ball and say, "This is stupid – why don't you get in the game?" I just said, "I'm not bothered about it, mate – I'm stopping *you* playing."

'He was the player and I was the stopper. And I won the day. I think it taught Gazza a lot. It was his first taste of real man-to-man marking – and it was something he had to find out about, especially at international level.

'Don Howe was pleased with the team's performance, but he wasn't happy I had grabbed Gascoigne. He praised me for my marking, but told me never to grab anyone like that again. He felt I could have done just as well without getting involved in all the verbals and off-the-ball stuff. I didn't argue with him, I was learning from Don at the time and respected all his experience. That's why I haven't grabbed anyone by the balls since.

'A girl had given Gascoigne some red roses before the game and one of the Wimbledon apprentices brought one into the dressing room for me. I wasn't on the sort of money he was earning, and couldn't afford roses, but I had to return the compliment. So I got a toilet brush out of the loo and told the apprentice to give that to him. The Newcastle lads were getting in the coach at the time, but I gather the joke went down quite well and Gazza laughed.

'I'm all for this Gazzamania stuff – it's great. He has earned everything he's getting.'

With Newcastle having met Wimbledon twice in the league and once in the Littlewoods Cup, that should have been the end of the unsavoury business, give or take the odd newspaper picture and story and complaining phone calls to Plough Lane from disgusted Gascoigne fans.

But, as fate would have it, Newcastle had to play Wimbledon again two weeks later, in the fifth round of the FA Cup. The match was overshadowed by mass media attention arising from the previous, headline-making encounter, and, not surprisingly, Paul was a bundle of nerves and played terribly in Newcastle's 3–1 defeat against the eventual Cup-winners.

Pickering says: 'We were psyched out of that game. On reflection, it was probably wrong to play Paul, but everyone was convinced his ability would overcome the problems. As it was, he went into his shell and the team didn't perform. After that, it was extremely difficult for us at away games. The Jones clash had given other teams the idea that if they could stop Paul Gascoigne playing, they could stop Newcastle playing.

'It worried Paul deeply, and we lost him for a while.'

For a young player already unhappy at Newcastle, the exit from the FA Cup – and, more particularly, the inconspicuous part he had played in the team's dismal performance – did not do much for Paul's morale. True, Newcastle were not involved in battling against relegation this time; but they were not chasing the championship title, either. The season drifted on to a somewhat meaningless finale against the less attractive sides in the First Division, with Newcastle destined to finish in a respectable, but uninspiring, spot in the table, just above halfway. After being hailed the relegation saviour only a year before, it had been a disappointing, and anti-climactic, season for Paul, with just seven goals from thirty-four hot and cold first-team appearances. And when the season finally drew to a close, and negotiations began for a new contract, Paul laid it on the line to agent Alistair Garvie: nothing he ever did was good enough for the fans on the St James's Park terraces, so he was not prepared to tolerate their stick any longer. They would have to find another whipping boy – or pay him enough to make him put up with them.

The club made one proposal after another. Paul turned them all down. 'He kept saying no, because he desperately wanted to leave,' says Garvie. 'He had been unhappy for a long time. The crowd were one thing, but I got the impression Paul also wanted to get away from the environment in which he was living.

'At that time, Paul had a bee in his bonnet that Newcastle had had him for nothing for two years before he signed his first contract. He felt he should be making fortunes and kept saying to me, "I hope you're going to make me a millionaire." It was all about money and Paul genuinely felt it would just come to him.

'The club he had set his heart on was Liverpool. He thought they were the best team in Britain and asked me to find out if they wanted to buy him. They were interested, but never spoke to Paul officially.

'Manchester United were interested, too, and we spoke to Alex Ferguson who said he had the money to meet Paul's demands. But Newcastle wouldn't let him speak with Paul officially, so nothing happened.'

For Willie McFaul, the whole saga was a painful experience: he liked Paul, admired and respected his ability and felt he was a tremendous asset for Newcastle. He wanted to keep him. But, deep down, he was always resigned to the inevitable.

'Paul always had big ideas, and there's no doubt he was always going to move on,' he says. 'The feelers started going out at the end of the previous season when he came back after injury and was playing brilliantly. I got a few phone calls from managers – Terry Venables among them – asking if Paul was for sale. But I always said no, and at that time I really did believe we could hang on to him.

'The following season many clubs were interested. Liverpool would have wanted Paul to stay at Newcastle another year to watch him develop – that's the way they work – but Alex Ferguson and others phoned me up. Only Spurs, though, actually put an offer on the table.

'We had been trying to negotiate a new contract with Paul personally for some months, but he wouldn't agree to anything and then his agent and other financial advisers took over.

'I didn't like the money men moving in and I tried to stop it. But it got to a stage when I had to hold my hands up and give in. No manager likes it when things reach that point.'

Alistair Garvie says that he got involved in the negotiations because Paul asked him to. Garvie, in turn, sought the help of his lawyer, Mel Stein – a Newcastle supporter he had met some twelve years before while assistant secretary at St James's Park – and an accountant, Leonard Lazarus.

The three men had three meetings with the Newcastle chairman, Gordon McKeag, and a director, George Forbes, at the Durham Hallgarth Manor. The first meeting, early in 1988, was to hear the offer Newcastle were making to Paul; the second was to discuss a counter-proposal; and the third to try to reach a compromise.

Today, Garvie says: 'The club approached Paul about a new contract in February when they saw how well he was playing. Paul still had more than a year of his contract to run, so he had no choice but to see what the club had to offer. They need not have offered him anything, of course, but when his contract ran out he would have been in a position, under the players' Freedom of Contract, to negotiate his own terms with other clubs.

'Paul just said to me, "Go in and see what happens." The club did offer a package worth about £1500 a week, but we turned it down because Paul was very unhappy at Newcastle. He felt he could get a lot more somewhere else. He fancied Liverpool more than anyone else, but no one from the club had made an offer. There was talk of Manchester United, but nothing concrete came from them either, although Alex Ferguson did say that money would not be a problem.

'Spurs came into the picture in late May after the third meeting at Hallgarth Manor failed to reach an agreement. Newcastle's directors decided they weren't going to keep Paul and gave Spurs permission to speak to him.'

Terry Venables, manager of the North London club, had wanted Gascoigne for some time. He had watched him himself, and had arranged for others to watch him, too. There was no question at all of the player's ability, but what concerned Venables was his reputation as a hot-headed, fiery-tempered individual. Before he asked Spurs to pay the £2 million Newcastle wanted, he needed the advice of someone who knew Paul well, both on and off the field. Who better than the England manager, Bobby Robson?

Bobby told him that the person who knew most about Paul Gascoigne the footballer was Dave Sexton, who had had the lad in the Under-21s for a year. Venables had known Sexton for twenty-seven years since they had been at Chelsea together – Venables as a player, and Sexton as coach.

One night in June he called his old pal, and they agreed to have lunch after a drink at London's Lancaster Hotel.

'Terry's main concern was what Gazza was like to handle, not how much it would cost to get him to Tottenham,' says Sexton. 'As a manager, you worry about personalities and what effect they will have on a team. You don't know if a player is nasty and will be a disruptive influence. Terry had some of those fears about Paul.

'I don't think he had met Paul then, and he wasn't sure if the boy was an out-and-out rotter or not. He had seen and read about his troubles on the field and the lack of discipline in his game, but he didn't know what to expect off the field.

'We both agreed Paul was worth the money, but the main question mark was getting the best out of him. Terry wasn't sure if he would settle down and improve at Tottenham.

'I said that if anyone could get Paul to improve, it was him. Terry is sympathetic, but firm, and young players respond to him. Paul was a vulnerable boy who needed guidance and he would respond, too.

'I said he was amiable and good-natured without a nasty streak. I also said he was perceptive and respectful and that Terry could get the best out of him. The problem would be fitting him into the framework of the team consistently.

'I didn't tell Terry anything new about Paul's game, but I helped put his mind at rest about what he was like to work with, and confirmed Terry could handle him.

'I didn't say "You should buy him" because that wasn't my decision. I just told him what I knew about Paul. Maybe it helped make up his mind.'

The speculation about Paul's future, inevitably, began to affect his end-of-season performance. He was getting advice from all quarters – his agents, the club management and other players – and he did not know which way to turn.

John Pickering, who watched it all from close range, says today, 'His mind must have been like a sponge. He was just a young local lad and it was such a big decision the pressure got to him.

'I noticed him getting quieter and quieter. He really didn't like people talking about him moving because, I think, it brought home that he had to make a decision. He wanted to do anything *but* speak about the situation. And when he had to speak about it, he wanted to speak only to those he was close to – no one else.

'The other players didn't give him a hard time, because each one knew he himself might be in a similar situation next year. They would take the mickey in various ways, though, and then Paul would go the other way and turn it round by snapping, "Yeah – that's right, I'm going . . . to a better club . . . to make more money. I'm in demand and I'll do what's right for me."

'But he never once said anything like that in a nasty way.

'The whole thing made him generally subdued and the only time he seemed to be himself was on the training ground when he was able to kick a ball around and vent whatever frustration and tension he was feeling.

'The pressure did get to him in matches, however, and towards the end of that season we didn't get the best out of him. It was a worrying time for us all.'

On 2 July Garvie got a phone call from St James's Park: the board had agreed to transfer Paul to Spurs for £2 million and now it was up to Garvie to agree the player's personal terms.

Garvie trusted Stein, the lawyer, and Lazarus, the accountant, to do the best deal for Paul with Spurs. But he wanted to be present when the transfer was officially signed in Stein's office in Regent's Park on 7 July and made arrangements to drive down the previous day. Spurs booked him into the West Lodge Park Hotel in Barnet, where Paul – in London for a charity event – was also staying. Those two days will not be remembered by Garvie as the least troublesome of his life.

'Paul didn't know precisely what fee had been agreed, but when he learned he went berserk,' says Garvie. 'He thought it was ridiculous that anyone should pay £2 million. He hated the idea.

'He had been acting strange, but now became even more difficult to deal with. It was hell between him and the national newspaper he was contracted to talk to. He didn't want to communicate with anyone but his mates, who had travelled from Newcastle to keep him company. They shouldn't have been there. They were not helping the situation.

'The afternoon before he signed, he flipped. He became impossible. He said he did not want Tottenham to have to pay the £2 million, but he couldn't do anything about it. Possibly he was frightened of being Britain's most expensive player. Certainly I didn't think he could handle it; it was too much for a young lad. All he wanted to do was get away from it and be with his mates. They just ate and drank in the hotel and got drunk. It was dreadful.

'On the day of the signing, he calmed down a little and we got a taxi into Central London. Before we went, we managed to persuade him that he had to speak to the reporter from the paper and he finally agreed.

'He didn't want Newcastle to have £2 million, because he felt they had had him for virtually nothing.

'The Spurs chairman, Irving Scholar, his personal assistant, Julia Masterman, Stein and Lazarus were waiting for us in Stein's office.

'Naturally, Paul was excited, but he wasn't ecstatic. Scholar's assistant took an instant dislike to him because, she confided to me later, he had been trying to chat her up behind Scholar's back. By the sound of it, he wasn't being very discreet and what he was saying wasn't very nice.

'"He's going to be trouble," she told me.

'We all sat at a big round table and Paul signed the necessary Football Association and Football League transfer forms. Newcastle had already signed one, and received half the money from Spurs. When it was all over, a bottle of champagne was opened but Paul did not want any; he did not want anything to drink at all.

'Then we went downstairs to have some photographs taken for the *Sun* newspaper. It was a steamy day and drizzling. We went over to a Rolls Royce, parked nearby, and the photographer did his stuff.

'Britain's most expensive footballer was standing there, moments after signing, but only a taxi driver recognized him. As he drove past, he shouted, "Good luck, Gazza." Paul waved back at him.

'Afterwards we went up to the office again, but Paul didn't say too much, and after a while went off to meet his friends at Madame Tussaud's. I drove home to Durham, thinking, "Thank God, it's all over."

'As I travelled up the motorway, I began thinking that Paul was a highly saleable asset, and I would have to make changes in my organization. I couldn't hope to control him from up north when he was in London, but I wasn't sure what to do. As it turned out, Stein and Lazarus would take over and I would have no part in Paul's future.

'The words of Irving Scholar's secretary kept coming back to me. "He'll be trouble." He had been for me. Would he be for Spurs, I wondered?'

Willie McFaul, who would be sacked as manager six months later, believes Newcastle did everything right and behaved properly in the Gascoigne affair.

'We got a bit of stick over the whole business, but I don't think Newcastle could have done much more to hang on to him,' he says today. 'It was a bad time for me, as manager, because I was facing losing other key players, too. And the hassle over Paul was made worse because we didn't know which club his advisers were aiming for him to go to. I don't think they knew; they were probably bouncing one off the other.

'Newcastle offered the lad a great deal of money, but he turned it down and it became a situation where the more we offered, the more they wanted. I don't know whether it was greed or simply a ploy to prevent Paul staying at Newcastle. Maybe they thought they would have a better commodity if he went elsewhere.

'The haggling went on and on and, finally, a joint decision had to be made. It was not a case of Paul's people turning down the Newcastle offer – it was a case of them demanding what I would call stupid money for a 21-year-old.

'It was as we were driving home after the third and last meeting that I knew in my heart that we had lost him. I felt we had gone as far as we could and I turned to the chairman and his fellow executives and said, "I don't think you can go any further, gentlemen. You should resign yourselves to the fact that we've lost him."

'The Newcastle public might think we should have stood on our heads to keep Paul, but, at the end of the day, he had to want to stay, and that feeling never came over. If he had wanted to stay, the money would not have mattered so much. The money – and it was a lot for the lad – would have more value in the North East than what he would get in the South. Looking back, I think the only thing that might have persuaded him to stay was if Newcastle were a club with a chance of honours.

'At the end of it all, we didn't know where he was going. One minute it was Manchester United, the next it was Liverpool. I don't think Paul had any idea himself. Certainly, I felt sure it was Old Trafford.

'Paul came to the ground one day when it was done and dusted, and I spotted him in the car park. I called him up to my office and said, "I wish you well. Keep your head."

'"You never know, boss," Paul replied, with the familiar grin. "I might be back in a couple of years."

'Then off he went, down the stairs, and as I watched him walk out of St James's Park, I felt sorry for the punters who were going to miss him, and a little for myself, too, because I felt Paul had let me down.'

12

For a young lad whose excitement had been limited to a couple of pints and a game of snooker at the Excelsior Working Men's Club, the first couple of months as a Tottenham Hotspur player were rather hairy. A script-writer would have been hard-pressed to write a more dramatic opening scenario.

Just three weeks after the transfer, Paul found himself in the centre of a storm, following a bust-up at a top London nightclub. Three times, Paul and a party of friends were asked to stop pestering people at the bar. But Paul, in merrier mood than usual, took no notice and, according to one female guest, kept strutting around like a chicken, sticking his chest out and generally making a nuisance of himself. The lady in question claimed Paul insulted her male companion because he had grey hair, nudged her arm when she tried to sip her drink, and shoved her around. The incident, predictably, made headlines in the tabloid press, prompting Venables to admit: 'Paul could prove to be a handful – on and off the pitch.'

Then word got out that, before he signed for Spurs, Paul had agreed to play for a team made up of mechanics and car salesmen against a showbiz XI in aid of a hospital in Melksham, Wiltshire. The match was due to be played shortly after the start of the season – the day after Spurs were to play Arsenal at White Hart Lane – and the or-ganizers admitted Paul was a 'mad fool' to risk playing. Venables pointed out the foolishness of playing and told Paul to forget it.

A couple of weeks later, on Tottenham's four-match, pre-season tour in Sweden, Venables banned Paul from leaving the team's hotel in Gonkoping, presumably to keep him out of trouble. But Britain's costliest player still managed to put himself in the headlines after a former model claimed he persuaded her to travel 180 miles to see him.

Venables, who knows a thing or two about footballers' high jinks from his days as a player, did his best to play down the alleged incident. What he found harder to ignore, one week later, was the dismal performance of his star-studded team in the opening match of the Wembley International Tournament.

It was the perfect stage for Paul to perform his enviable repertoire; a heaven-sent opportunity for him to prove that Venables' faith and, more particularly, that much-publicized price tag, were justified. And what could have made the taste of success even sweeter was that the opposition were Tottenham's North London rivals, Arsenal.

Sadly, what Paul had hoped would be a day of triumph turned into misery as Spurs were slaughtered 4–0, with the Arsenal fans greeting each goal with the taunting chants, 'What's the score, Fat Boy?' and, predictably, 'What a waste of money.'

Normally one of the game's great communicators, Venables was press-shy after the match, preferring to hold a conference himself with the team at their hotel.

It was a gloomy start for Paul, who, only a few days before the Wembley match, had inspired Spurs skipper Gary Mabbutt to liken him to Glenn Hoddle. 'Gazza could be a hero at White Hart Lane for the next ten years,' he predicted.

Heroes, however, need luck. And there was not any around for Paul when the season opened on 27 August. He had been looking forward to repairing the Wembley damage to his reputation, if not his pride, in his league debut at home to Coventry. But, astonishingly, the game was called off the day before, because one of Tottenham's new grandstands was not finished and therefore did not meet safety standards. Both Venables and Paul admitted it was a bad blow – the worst thing that could have happened in terms of Paul's first league outing. For it left him with the awesome prospect of making that nerve-tingling debut in front of the fans who had loved and hated him throughout those bitter-sweet years before the Mars Bar Kid became the Superstar.

If the home-coming was not daunting enough, first Mirandinha, then Willie McFaul, put the boot in to stoke up the red-hot tension the tabloids were putting into the game. The Brazilian, a friend off the field, blazed, 'We're doing all right without Gazza.' And McFaul, at the centre of an amazing summer transfer merry-go-round in which £6 million changed hands, urged his new-look team to prove, 'We don't need Paul Gascoigne.'

Paul himself hit back by accusing Newcastle of forcing him to leave by lacking ambition. And he promised that the fans would see a different player from the one ridiculed by gloating Arsenal fans at Wembley.

The truth, however, is that Paul was in an impossible 'no-win' situation at St James's Park that warm September afternoon. If he did the business and spurred Tottenham to victory, he would be the villain to home fans; if he played badly and Spurs won, he would still be scorned as a £2 million flop; if he played well, but Newcastle won, he would be jeered as a loser. Chris Waddle, who had gone through it all himself, warned Paul it would be bad, but nothing could have prepared Paul for the intensity of the Newcastle fans' hostility and derision for more than two hours that day.

It began when he arrived in the team coach, to be greeted with shouts of 'Judas' and 'traitor' from resentful Geordies. And it went on throughout the game, during which he was taunted incessantly and bombarded with Mars bars, sold from a trestle table outside a garage near the ground.

When he was substituted thirteen minutes from time, supposedly suffering from cramp, the one-time idol of the
Gallowgate End was jeered all the way to the dugout.

For two hours after the final whistle, fifty or so Newcastle
supporters – a cross-section of pimply youths, giggling
schoolgirls and middle-aged autograph hunters – waited with
scrapbooks and Instamatics, but Paul had left by an entrance
on the other side of the ground. That sad and shadowy exit,
perhaps, said more about his return home than anything else.

Willie McFaul remembers the day well. 'We had to
hound Paul and stop him doing things in the match,' he
says. 'I think he felt over-awed at being at St James's Park
again and went into his shell.

'Before the game, I remember I came out of our dressing
room at the same time Terry Venables came out of theirs.
We were standing there in our shirt-sleeves, waiting for
the lads to come out, and I said, "How ya getting on?" He
raised his eyebrows. "What d'ya think?" he said.

'"How is he doing for you?" I asked.

'"I'm not sure yet," Terry said, and I could sense the
apprehension.

'"Terry, he *can* play," I said. "He's just a bit difficult to
work with."

'Terry didn't say much. He appreciated that I knew the
situation, but I don't think he wanted me to give him any
of the background. He wanted to find out for himself.'

Despite his tepid display in that baptism of fire, the
tabloids began what was to be a prolonged and insistent
clamour for Paul to be given his first full England cap.
And Bobby Robson seemed to be swayed when, a couple
of days later, he included Paul in his 22-man squad to meet
Denmark in a friendly at Wembley on 14 September.

Paul got the news from Chris Waddle at White Hart
Lane after the squad was announced the following Tuesday. 'Congratulations,' Chris said. 'You're in. All the best.'

For Paul, it was the greatest thrill of his life; what he

had dreamt of from the moment he first kicked a ball. And he readily acknowledged the debt he owed Dave Sexton, whose advice about his on-field behaviour had 'well and truly registered'.

Paul had been hurt by many of the insults hurled at him, but they had made him stronger, ready for the challenge. He was winning the seemingly endless battle of the bulge, which, he said, showed how determined he was to succeed, not only as a Tottenham player, but also as an England one.

In the end, Paul did not make the starting line-up against Denmark, and today Bobby Robson says, 'He was bubbly and thought he was going to play, but I didn't pick him. The Press were putting me under pressure to experiment, but we had lost three games on the trot and it was not the time to experiment – we needed a win.

'It was quite amazing. When Gazza played in the Wembley tournament, certain newspapers called him a £2 million flop. Yet, a few weeks later, the same people were saying he's an England saviour.

'Gazza was a rich, rare talent and I was sure his time would come. But only when I thought he was ready. He certainly wasn't then. He was fat and played only twenty minutes in each half before fading out of games. He would make a clever pass or score a goal and the papers would scream, "Pick Gazza!" What, on one pass, one goal, playing up at Leicester or wherever, when I'd be thinking about playing Brazil or West Germany!

'When I watched Gazza, I didn't focus on the one great pass or the goal that the Press picked up on – I watched his whole game and, quite honestly, he wasn't ready to play a real, responsible role in midfield. Bryan Robson was always going to be the first choice and next was, who would play with him. Robson scores goals, and if he's up in the box doing that we needed someone to be in position. Gazza couldn't do that. If Robson went up front, Gazza would be flying up there with him.

'So, as the papers kept on and on, I just kept my head. I told myself, don't listen. Do it yourself. Sit down and take stock of the situation and make the right decision for the country, not the *Sun* or the *Mirror*. I was very conscious that it would be wrong to burden a kid still coming to terms with a change of club and a huge transfer fee by picking him for the team. But, that September, I made up my mind that he would be in the twenty-two, subject to injury and decent progression. I wasn't sure the lad could do it at international level, but I still felt he was the sort of player who might make the difference and swing a vital game – someone I could put on late and get us out of trouble.'

Against the Danes, Bobby was not in trouble. But shortly before the end – with England winning 1–0 – he decided to give Paul a run-out. An expectant buzz hummed around the ground as Paul trotted on to the pitch to replace Peter Beardsley. For the £2 million man of the moment, the reluctant hero who just wanted to play football, it was an appearance on the highest international stage.

Wembley, deprived of an entertainer for so long, welcomed him warmly.

At White Hart Lane, however, the natives of North London were getting restless. Paul and the other big-money signing, Paul Stewart from Manchester City, were not working the promised magic, and Spurs were languishing – ironically, with Newcastle – near the foot of the First Division. Paul came in for his fair share of criticism, both from the fans and his manager: while everyone loved his flair and his desire to entertain, they were bothered by his over-confidence, which had cost goals against Charlton and Southampton. The honeymoon period was over. The Tottenham faithful wanted a return to the glory days – and a return on the millions the club had spent trying to achieve them. The season was barely three months old, but there was talk of a crisis, made worse by an embarrassingly inept Littlewoods Cup display against Third Division Notts County. Only Paul's magical eightieth minute curler into the top corner saved Spurs' blushes that October night.

At least one fan kept a sense of humour amid the gloom surrounding White Hart Lane. Outside the ground, a poster offered the encouraging message, 'Jesus Saves'. The witty fan's equally optimistic offering scrawled underneath said, 'But Gazza scores from the rebound.'

There was talk of a crisis, too, on Tyneside, where Willie McFaul was facing the sack for Newcastle's dreadful start to the season. Unhesitatingly, Paul leaped to the defence of his former boss, with a stinging attack on the club's directors, whose lack of ambition, he repeated, had driven him away from St James's Park.

Never one to miss the chance of a wind-up, Paul found himself in the headlines yet again six weeks later, after Spurs had, somewhat surprisingly, got through the third round of the Littlewoods Cup after two tense ties with Blackburn Rovers. The trouble started when Blackburn's central defender, Colin Hendry, slated Paul after a goalless draw at Tottenham. Paul, who had had to suffer bad jokes and cruel jibes aimed at him and his rock-bottom side all season, did not like it. 'It's out of order for a player from a lower division to put the boot in when you're on the floor,' he said. And when Spurs won the replay 2–1, he took pleasure in taunting Hendry in a revengeful verbal attack – and went looking for him in a Blackburn club, demanding to know, 'Where's the big mouth who said we were useless?'

Blackburn boss, Don Mackay, did not like it and steamed into Paul, saying, 'If players go around like that, I don't know what the game is coming to.'

With Spurs in such trouble in the league, Paul's off-the-field skirmishes were not appreciated by the Tottenham management; and it was, perhaps, fortuitous that a few days later Paul had more to occupy his mind than baiting a Third Division club. He was on the substitutes' bench for an England game against Saudi Arabia in Riyadh, on 16 November – with an outside chance of getting on.

It was a tight match – perfect for Paul to be thrown in late to make the difference and swing the game England's way. Bobby Robson, true to his gut feeling about the lad, did just that. With half an hour to go, he turned to Paul on the bench. 'Get warmed up, son. You're going on.'

Today, Bobby remembers the moment with a smile. 'Gazza was up in a flash,' he says. '"Put me on now, boss, and I'll get you a goal – I will," he said.

'He didn't, as it happens, but that was an indication of his confidence and awareness of what he's capable of. Others would have got up quietly and got on with their warm-up, but not Gazza – he's telling me he's going to get me a goal!'

It was this positive attitude that endeared Gazza to Bobby, as much as the lad's patience and understanding when he, like millions of other people, thought he should be in the team.

Bobby says, 'I would generally call the squad into the centre circle at our training ground the day before the match and tell them who was in and who wasn't. There would be nine or so disappointed players, so Gazza wasn't alone. He *thought* he should be in the team, but when he learned he wasn't, he didn't say anything or react in a particular way, or blame me. I could tell he was disappointed, but he would just look at me and give a sorrowful smile. He never came to me and said, "Hey, you should put me in the team."

'On a couple of occasions in those early days, when he'd just broken into the squad, I would take him to one side on the training ground or at the hotel, and tell him a day before anyone else that he wouldn't be playing on Wednesday.

'I would say, "You're here, you're in the squad, and that's what matters. I'm looking after you. Learn to behave, and watch Robson and Shilton and Butcher play and listen to them – they'll bring you on."

'I didn't single out players very often to tell them they weren't playing, but I did with Gazza, because I knew I had to encourage him, not knock him down. I knew, ultimately, it would come his way and I felt I had to tell him that. And, probably, because he is so much more sensitive.

'He always took the news well. He'd listen to what I was saying and come back with, "Oh, aye, all right . . . okay . . . I know. But when I get in, I'll *be* in – and you won't want me out." He was so confident in his ability, he was really saying, "Once you put me in the team, I'll be so good, you won't be able to deny me any more."

'I would say, "I know you will, son. And when you *are* ready, I'll pick you. I'll make sure you get your chance."'

On that sultry Arabian night in November 1988, that chance seemed distant indeed. For Robson returned to a roasting. He had given in, as the newspapers urged, and experimented with five young players. But because England had been held to a 1–1 draw he was castigated, yet again, for doing the wrong thing. If his new-look team had hammered the Saudis, however, the headlines would have been, 'We told you so.' Bobby could not win.

During his first few months as a Tottenham player, Paul had been staying at a hotel on the borders of London and Hertfordshire which made it clear that guests were expected to be quiet and responsible. This proved somewhat difficult for Paul and the Gateshead mates he regularly invited down to ease his loneliness. With Spurs picking up the tab for all Gazza's expenses, it was not unknown for them to stay up late, drinking at the hotel bar, sometimes splashing out on champagne. This, inevitably, led to high jinks that did not go down at all well with the hotel management. After one particularly noisy, high-spirited spree, during which a fire extinguisher was let off, the hotel complained to Tottenham and Gazza was warned to cool it.

It was a lengthy and eventful stay, and it was no doubt with relief that hotel staff greeted the news, just before Christmas, that Gazza's plans to buy a house in Clyde Road, Hoddesdon, Hertfordshire, were nearly finalized and he would soon be moving in.

Luxurious and convenient though the hotel was, Paul felt more at home in Gateshead, and he would drive there at every opportunity, even if it meant him getting up at dawn to drive back in time for training.

On 1 December, however, these journeys home were seriously hit when Gazza was banned from driving. His solicitor's plea that Paul had a lot on his mind with contract negotiations the previous May cut no ice with the magistrates at Blaydon, Tyne and Wear, who banned Paul for six months and fined him £75 for driving at 97 mph on the A69 at Eighton Banks, Gateshead. Travelling home that Christmas, however, was not something he had considered, since Spurs had a Boxing Day match against Luton; so Paul had to miss out on Christmas at home for the first time in his life.

There was plenty of festive spirit at Tottenham, though. After that awful start, the team had put together some good results and, from being a club on the brink of crisis, they were ending 1988 as possible championship contenders. Paul's irrepressible style had affected everyone at the club, from players and coaches to office staff, and he went into that Luton game with a worthy accolade from Venables's close friend and assistant, Allan Harris.

'It's like having Les Dawson at the club,' said the likeable former QPR player, who had loyally assisted Venables at London clubs and in Barcelona. 'Paul's a really funny man – joking and pulling faces all the time. He gets up to all sorts of nonsense and some bosses wouldn't have him

149

because he's a disruptive influence. But there's not a malicious bone in his body and you end up forgiving him for everything. There are times when you want to get hold of him and give him a right talking to. But you don't because of the sort of bloke he is.

'And his attitude is great. He's the sort of player who wants to turn out, even if he's got a slight knock. He's a real character – the type that people want to see. And that's good for football.'

No one appreciated more than Bobby Robson just how good Gazza was going to be. Which is why, that December, he announced plans to create an England B team – a much-needed stepping stone between the Under-21s and the senior side for gifted young players such as Gazza.

Revealing the plan, Bobby said, 'If I were a club manager with around sixty matches a season, it would be easy to introduce bright young kids, but with just eight internationals a season, I'm restricted in how much I dare experiment. I'm in a cleft stick, particularly as players can't increase their education in Europe because of the club ban.'

An England B team, he said, would be perfect to accommodate players like Gazza. And he went on the record about Gazza's precocious talent, saying he could be exceptional as a player – 'another great like Best and Law and Charlton, who all had the same burning self-belief.'

The Boxing Day match had left Paul with an ankle injury that ruled him out of the first three games of the New Year. But that was nothing compared to the knock his pride took when former Newcastle chairman Stan Seymour launched an attack on him publicly, calling him 'George Best without brains'.

Gazza, stung by the snipe, hit back immediately, accusing the Newcastle board of being 'brainless' to sell him.

'What brains has Seymour got?' he fumed. 'He was involved in selling me to Spurs with a year of my contract to run. He's the one who's brainless. Newcastle got £2 million for me and are near the bottom of the First Division. That shows you all you want to know about directors at the club. They're clueless.'

And he pointed out for good measure that, unlike George Best, he had never been locked in a prison cell or done a runner from training or matches.

Ironically, the verbal punch-up came shortly before Gazza was due to return to the North East for a game at Middlesbrough – his first full league match since Boxing Day. Predictably, the row added to the highly charged tension and Paul was pelted with Mars bars, pork pies and coins by an angry Ayresome Park crowd. Having run that particular gauntlet in even more hostile circumstances in September, Paul was not fazed and responded amusingly by unwrapping one of the chocolate missiles and pretending to eat it. One of the noisiest in the crowd, near the front, was wearing glasses, so Paul instinctively seized an opportunity: he took an imaginary pair of spectacles from his shorts, and put them on. Then he promptly walked into an imaginary lamp-post and fell down on the pitch. It amused the crowd and took some of the heat out of the situation!

Four days later, in London, the laugh-in continued at a Press reception at the Tower Hotel to announce a football boot sponsorship. The deal, enthused the manufacturers, could boost Paul's off-the-field earnings to more than £1 million, but the kid who once called his cheap and battered soccer boots his 'Woolworths specials' took it all in his jaunty stride. Taking one of the red, blue, yellow and green boots from Brooks director Mel Batty, he wise-cracked, 'They're lovely, Mel. Do I get a pair of sunglasses to go with them?' Asked where he got his outrageous 'naked lady' tie, Paul quipped, 'I came last in a competition at Tottenham. This was the booby prize.'

Had he tested the boots? Paul glanced at Mel Batty and said, 'No – I'm leaving that to Nora Batty.' What are your ambitions for the season? someone asked. 'To sell as many boots as possible,' Paul responded with a grin.

And so it went on. The media, hungry for morsels of Gazza mouthings, ate up greedily everything he gave them. But, at the end of it all, Paul seemed quite unmoved by the hoo-ha and even less excited by all the talk of him becoming a millionaire.

'I have people I trust looking after my money and I haven't seen my bank statement for seven months,' he admitted. 'I have no idea what I've got.'

What did concern him, however, was the hint that what was happening to him had happened – with disastrous consequences – to George Best.

The boot makers were hailing Gazza as the biggest name in football since the legendary Manchester United star. But Gazza wanted everyone to know he was not going to finish up like Best.

'There's no way I'm not going to be able to handle the pressure,' he vowed. 'I've just got too big a heart to let any problems get on top of me.' And, referring to the knockers who were still predicting he would fall flat on his face, Paul said, 'Whatever they want to say, I've heard it all before and I'll probably hear it all again. But it will never get me down.'

What *was* getting him down was his right ankle. He had had stitches put in after getting another knock at Middlesbrough, but they had burst open in training – and now, just ten days before England were to play Greece in Athens, Paul resigned himself to missing the game, even if selected.

In the event, he was not even picked as sub; the week before the Wednesday match, Bobby Robson made it clear that while he agreed Paul had the talent to be an England player, he still did not have the head for it. Someone who *did* have the head for it, of course, was Bryan Robson, and Paul had an ideal opportunity to show what he could do against him three days before the England squad flew off. For Tottenham were playing Manchester United in a live TV match at Old Trafford. It was Paul's first full game for Spurs in front of the cameras, and he went into it revealing that the England skipper was the player he had admired – 'the one I look up to' – since playing in a Newcastle side hammered 4–0 by United.

Paul said, 'As we left the pitch that day, my own captain, Glenn Roeder, grabbed me, pointed in Bryan's direction, and said, "That's what you have to aim for."

'He told me the day I reached the standard set by Bryan Robson, that's when I would have cracked it. I've never forgotten those words.

'Forget all the talk about Vinny Jones being the player to frighten the life out of you – they don't come any harder than Robson.'

The following Thursday, while the England players were in Athens celebrating a 2–1 win, Paul was in London, contemplating an appearance of a totally different, and more serious, nature. His outburst at former Newcastle chairman Stan Seymour had offended the FA, and, though neither Newcastle nor Seymour had complained, Paul was charged with bringing the game into disrepute and told to appear before a disciplinary commission at the FA's Lancaster Gate headquarters later that month.

The week before the hearing, Paul did his England chances no favours with a petulant performance for Tottenham in a 1–1 home draw with Charlton, watched by Bobby Robson. The England manager, who had said he wanted Gazza 'to get his head together' before he picked him for England, saw the gifted Geordie react angrily to several bad fouls and get booked for swearing. Although Venables defended Gazza, saying that referees should protect high-quality players, the indiscipline of a player whose temperament was notoriously questionable did not impress Robson at all. The latest misdemeanour took Paul past twenty-one disciplinary points, which meant a two-match ban, and one wondered if, at international level at least, the talent would be enough to outweigh the temper.

As Dave Sexton recalls today, 'If I saw Paul play in the

League and he got into trouble, or if I picked up the papers and he was all over the back pages for getting involved in some bother, I'd be in despair. I would think, Oh, no – that's another nail in his coffin. All the arguments and the bookings made me question whether he could live up to international football, temperamentally. And, yes, I must admit I did think at times that he wouldn't make it, and wouldn't get his chance.

'His behaviour was always the main worry; it was always that which would let him down.

'When we had an England Under-21 game or tour coming up, I would speak to Bobby Robson on the phone three or four times a week, or we would have dinner. Paul wasn't the focus of our conversations all the time, but he did come up a lot.

'It was always a question of the talent and the discipline. We would ask ourselves if, by playing him, it would be a case of "strength or disrupt". Experienced players do not like a young boy to come in and take liberties. The A team needs stability and when young fellas come in, the first question the senior players ask is, "Is this kid reliable or a flash in the pan?" Paul could be brilliant. But he could also be unreliable. He needed to be both brilliant and reliable to be in the England team.'

Don Howe, too, was irritated and frustrated by Paul's lack of reliability. 'We all knew he had the individual skill, but he was erratic and wouldn't hold his position. It was a case of, "Where's Gazza now – oh, he's outside right," and "Where's Gazza now – oh, he's outside left." He didn't follow through the instructions he got in the Under-21s, didn't play to the responsibilities of the team.'

Happily for Paul, the FA let him off with a warning, with a promise to write to Stan Seymour, asking him why he described Paul as 'a George Best without brains'. It was a minor victory for Paul, who believed he was in the right because the former Newcastle chairman had fired the first shot. And, still angered at the attack, Paul warned that if the abuse continued, he would retaliate. 'I have a suitcase full of stories that I will expose and embarrass the Newcastle directors,' he warned.

All in all, it had been a fraught February. But there were at least two bright spots for Paul as the run-in to the end of the season began: even though his ankle injury meant he had completed only two games since before Christmas, an unbeaten spell had lifted Spurs well clear of the relegation zone; and, on the home front, his elder sister, Anna, landed an acting part in a TV drama.

Paul was not in the team that beat Albania 2–0 in a World Cup qualifying match in Tirana on 8 March. But he was in the squad that went there, and Bobby Robson remembers it as the trip where Gazza was accepted as one of the boys by senior England players.

'He became really popular with the lads out there,' Bobby remembers. 'I think it began during a training session in the ground. There were about 7,000 Albanians watching and, after giving them a shooting display, Gazza decided to put on a goalkeeping one. He had all the players, and even me and Don, in hysterics. He was play-acting, performing as a keeper. He would go for the ball, but let it through his hands, or instead of saving it, he would head it away at the last second, or dive the wrong way. We were all laughing our stocking-tops off. He was terrific and had the crowd loving it as well. He did a wonderful job that day and was great to have around the rest of the trip.'

With his cheeky face, madcap personality and sunny outlook on life now an enjoyable part of the England set-up, it seemed only a question of time before Paul got his chance.

For Bobby Robson, however, the on-field tantrums and that irritating, niggling, frustrating worry about the lad's reliability kept getting in the way of pencilling his name on the team-sheet.

And then, four weeks before the return match with Albania, Paul stormed back into the revitalized Spurs team at Luton and scored a spectacular goal after beating two players in a dazzling 45-yard run.

Would that, the media and the nation's football lovers wondered, be enough to put him in the Wembley line-up?

13

It wasn't. Robson, happy with the midfield performances of Neil Webb, Bryan Robson and David Rocastle in Tirana, was not prepared to take any chances, despite the weak opposition; but Paul did find himself elevated from goalkeeping clown to the substitutes' bench.

And then, with twenty-four minutes to go, England found themselves 3–0 up and looking for more. Bobby decided to let his exuberant, if mischievous, puppy off his lead to enjoy himself.

It was twenty-four minutes that sent 60,000 Wembley faithfuls home with a smile on their faces, and cynical football reporters reaching for rarely used superlatives.

Robson will never forget that night of 26 April.

'I didn't want to risk Gazza at first,' he admits. 'The match was still competitive, but safe. We got to 3–0 with just over twenty minutes to go and I thought: We can't lose now – let's chuck him on. Whatever he does, he won't make us lose 4–3. If he is a luxury, then this is the time to enjoy that luxury; let's see the good aspects of him.

'I didn't want to lose the belly of the team in midfield, so I decided to take off Rocastle, who was playing wide on the right. Before calling him off, I turned to Gazza and said, "Look, you're in a nice position. You don't have to worry about the result – the game's safe. Go out and enjoy yourself. Get the ball as much as you can and attack. But"

156

– and I stressed this – "keep to the right-hand side, where David was, to keep the shape of the team." It was important, so I said it a couple of times. "Don't forget – keep to this side; operate from here. Keep the shape and be sensible. You'll enjoy it."

'So Gazza went on, didn't he? And the first thing he did, he disobeyed me. He went straight across to the left-hand side of the pitch and started playing with his mate, Waddle. They're both Geordie lads, and very thick. They get along very well.

'It probably wasn't so much disobeying me – more a case of everything I'd said going in one ear and straight out the other. He just forgot everything about my instructions.

'I remember turning to Don Howe and saying, "Look at that silly bugger. He's as daft as a fucking brush, isn't he? I told him to play over here and now he's gone off to play with his mate. He's as daft as a brush."

'I got up from the bench and waved at Gazza and shouted, "Here, Gazza, get over here. *This* side." He did come over, but then started playing all over the shop.

'Funnily enough, he got a goal from where I'd told him to play. He picked up the ball on the right, beat a man, maybe two, and scored a remarkable goal with his left foot.

'The "daft as a brush" thing was just something I said to Don that night; no one else heard it. When I saw Gazza pranking around at a training session some time later, I said, "You're as daft as a brush, you are, Gazza," and, the next day, he turned up with a little sweeping brush stuck down his sock. It was really funny and raised a helluva laugh with the other lads. The next day, of course, it was headlines.'

Bobby's description was apt and amusing; it even inspired a book of Gazza jokes, with *Daft as a Brush* as the title. But, despite that brush-in-the-sock joke, Gazza himself did not find the manager's view of him very funny at all. In fact, says Tony Dorigo, he was very bothered by it.

'The comment came at a time then Gazza really wanted to be in the team, and "daft" wasn't the impression he wanted people to have of him,' says Tony. 'He certainly didn't like to have the boss thinking of him in that way. Gazza made light of it because that's his way, but I know from talking to him that he was angry and annoyed.

'He wasn't too happy about certain things in the Press, but thought they didn't matter too much. If the manager thought him a silly idiot, though, that was quite different. He wondered what chance did he have. The "daft as a brush" thing really got to him – and fired him up. It might actually have got him in order slightly. He was always a determined guy, but that made him want to prove, more than ever, to Robson and the Press what he could do.'

Not surprisingly, Fleet Street's football reporters ladled their euphoria heavily with hyperbole after the Albania match. Gazza had played for just twenty-four minutes against a well-beaten side with tired legs and their minds on the next flight to Tirana. But it was more than enough for newspapers which had been telling Bobby Robson for months that Gazza was the player to put flair and smiles back into English football.

Never keen to let the facts spoil a good story, the tabloids made much of Bobby Robson's extravagant praise for Gazza – that he reminded him of George Best and could become another Platini – but a lot less of the flaw still worrying the manager: the lad's lack of responsibility to the team.

In truth, nothing had really changed. Robson always knew that Gazza was a 'rich and rare talent' who could go on in the last twenty minutes and make the crowd gasp with audacious skill and a spectacular goal. And he always knew Gazza was unreliable and likely to drop his team-mates in it by doing something quite silly.

What that match did prove conclusively to Bobby was

that, in Gazza, he had an exciting challenge – 'the challenge of producing an outstanding world player to do for England what Platini did for France'.

It was at that time that he and Don Howe realized they could not leave Gazza out of their World Cup plans.

'We felt we'd have to take him, because in a year's time he might be really something,' Bobby says today. 'We didn't think he'd be in the team, but we thought that, with twenty minutes to go in a game, he was the sort of player who could get us a goal.'

Someone who did not share Bobby's optimism of Gazza's future was the man who masterminded England's 1966 World Cup triumph, Sir Alf Ramsey. He was not impressed that Robson talked of Gazza in the same breath as Best or Platini.

'Gazza is too selfish . . . and I am definitely not confident he can do it at the top level,' said Sir Alf. The former England manager had always been immediately suspicious of 'crowd pleasers' and admitted he never encouraged them in his sides. 'I always believed those stars with a high profile and brimming with outrageous ability were also inconsistent – and the first to let the team down,' he said. 'So far, in my opinion, Gascoigne is not an international player. He lacks discipline and is a free spirit who needs to be controlled more.'

Bobby Robson shared that last sentiment. His lovable puppy called Gazza was a joy to have around, but he had been naughty, and would have to learn to behave and obey before being let off his lead again.

The next chance for Gazza to show he had learned from his Albania experience came in Winterthur, Switzerland, on 16 May – the first of two matches for Robson's newly formed England B team. But Paul went into the match with a stern warning from manager Dave Sexton and Robson: behave – or you'll be substituted. Gazza, who had been booked eight times that season, got the message and turned in an impeccable performance, crowned with a stunning solo goal that eclipsed even his Albania effort. He picked up the ball just outside the centre circle, strolled past three Swiss players – twice with neat double shuffles – rounded the keeper and tapped the ball into an empty net.

After a dull first half, the goal gave the tiny 950 crowd – and England bosses – something to cheer.

'It was a fantastic goal,' Robson later enthused. 'The game was crying out for a bit of individual flair.'

Gazza seemed to have learned his lesson in disobeying orders. Although he struggled in that tedious first forty-five minutes in an unfamiliar role wide on the right, he showed patience and composure – and not a little discipline. No wonder Robson said, 'This was a learning process for Gazza and it was a highly professional performance.'

Predictably, the Press latched on to the goal and Gazza's more mature performance, and began suggesting that he was the man for the midfield job in the crucial World Cup qualifier against Poland at Wembley on 3 June. Coolly, Robson replied that the lad had to prove he was better than Bryan Robson, Neil Webb and Steve McMahon, and he had not done it.

'It was frustrating,' Bobby recalls, 'but I knew he had to learn more about the game and needed time. He was with a good club and Terry Venables was working on his game and trimming him down, but Gazza was still fading from games and doing irresponsible things – like losing the ball in key areas and making the odd careless pass where it hurt.

'I was watching him more than any England manager had ever watched any player, and out of all those games I didn't ever think Gazza was not going to make an England player. But I did keep wishing he would master the *two* aspects of football: what you do when you've got the ball, and what you do when you haven't. It's not so important if you're a winger, but if you play in the heart of midfield – the engine room – you've got to be that way. I knew Gazza had the talent and the football brain, but I didn't know if he had the responsibility. It was all just a bit of a laugh to him, really.'

So, as the crunch first World Cup match with Poland loomed nearer, Robson knew that, despite the Press clamour for Gazza, there would be no place for him at Wembley, not even on the substitutes' bench.

It was going to be a hard, tough, tight match on which England's World Cup hopes might depend. And one that needed experience more than exuberance to see them through.

But before that crucial encounter there were two Wembley matches with less at stake – Rous Cup games against Chile and Scotland. To the delight of the Press and an expectant sporting nation, Robson gave Gazza the nod to play in the No. 8 shirt on the right side of midfield against the South Americans.

Before the match, Robson quipped, 'We'll have to nail Gazza to the ground.' But Gazza, for once, wasn't in the mood for jokes.

'Please take me seriously,' he pleaded. 'I know what I've got to do and I'll play any way and anywhere the boss asks me to.

'Against Albania, I got carried away. I wanted the ball all the time and felt tremendous. But I know what to do this time. I'm not in the team to put smiles on people's faces – I'm in because of the way I've been playing for Spurs.'

The game ended in a stifling o–o draw. But Gazza played well and pleased the crowd. He behaved well, too, and pleased Robson. The mischievous, ubiquitous puppy, his master was relieved to discover, had been brought to heel, with no damage to his personality. Now, anything was possible.

14

Before a ball was kicked in the next league season, Gazza was in mischief again – off the field and on it.

In the second week of June, after an operation on his injured ankle, Gazza went to Newcastle's training ground for a bit of shooting practice. But it was with a newly acquired 12-bore shotgun, not his boots, and police were called to give him and three friends a talking to.

Groundsman David Orchard, who was there at the time, recalls: 'Gazza and his mates had a big clay-pigeon machine and asked if they could practise with it on the ground. No one was around at the time, so I said okay, but it was nothing to do with me if anyone complained.

'Gazza shot at the clay pigeons from the machine for a few minutes, but then saw some real ones on the grass and took pot shots at them. He killed a couple, which was all right by me because the pigeons are a nuisance, eating the seed from the football pitches.

'He'd shot a dozen or so rounds, mainly at the clay pigeons, when two policemen from the local station drove into the ground.

'One of them said, "We might have known it would be you, Gazza," and told him that every police car in Newcastle would be there in five minutes if he didn't put the gun away.

'Gazza apologized and said he thought he was allowed to shoot because he was more than fifty yards from the nearest house. Thankfully, I'd got rid of the dead pigeons.

'The police gave Gazza and his mates a good talking to and I thought no more about it, but then it was headlines in the local evening paper and I got a right rollocking from the club's general manager, Russell Cushing. All I could say was, "You know what Gazza's like."'

Gazza, slimmer than ever thanks to intensive summer training and a controlled diet, hit the headlines again in a pre-season friendly against Glasgow Rangers at Ibrox Park – but not in the way either his Spurs manager or Bobby Robson wanted. He was booked for spitting in the face of Rangers' midfield player Ian Ferguson, in an ill-tempered match which Spurs lost 1–0. And to make matters worse, Gazza accidentally clashed heads with team-mate Gary Lineker, causing the striker to need six stitches.

Venables, understandably annoyed, made it clear, in his no-nonsense East London style, that his £2 million star should grow up. Gazza responded by saying he *had* grown up a lot since his move from Newcastle and was looking forward to proving it by being more responsible on the pitch during the coming season.

'I had a lot of problems last season,' he said. 'I had difficulty getting a house sorted out and had to live in a hotel. But now I am settled into my new home and want to help Spurs win the title and push my England claim further. Now, I can handle anything.'

What he could *not* handle, in only the second match of the season, however, was fellow Spurs star Gary Stevens trying to prevent him being sent off in a midweek game at Everton. Gazza, who had been booked in the fourth minute for a foul on Mike Newell – his second caution in two games – was later sent crashing in a tit-for-tat tackle. As Gazza got up and went for the Everton man, Stevens ran between them to try to calm his team-mate down, but Gazza turned on him, grabbing him by the throat and pushing him away. The referee called Gazza over after booking Newell, but allowed him to continue after a long lecture.

It was an ugly incident that Gazza regretted almost immediately, and he later apologized to Stevens. But it demonstrated that no matter how much Gazza felt he had matured, he clearly hadn't. Not that he felt he was entirely to blame; over-enthusiastic referees, he believed, saw him as an easy target.

'It seems that I am a name and there to be shot at,' he said. 'I'm getting booked the moment I step out of line, while some players can do virtually what they like. Well, in future, some people are going to be disappointed because every time I'm whacked, I'll get up and just smile.'

As Gazza went into the third match of the season, against Manchester City, facing a hat-trick of cautions, Venables himself made a passionate appeal to referees not to 'crucify' his star signing. 'Paul's name and reputation are going before him,' said the Spurs manager. 'He is making an effort with his temperament, but is still getting done by refs. He has got so much to offer and no one wants to see that knocked out of him. As long as he doesn't go beyond the laws of the game, Paul shouldn't be targeted.'

At Maine Road, Gazza was not booked. But he did get a ticking-off from the referee – for his sense of humour! City defender Paul Lake, who had somewhat prominent ears, tried to put Gazza off his game by continually calling him 'Fatty', so the Spurs man responded by pulling his ears out, Dumbo style. The referee did not see the funny side. But Gazza had the last laugh, scoring his first goal of the season to earn Spurs a valuable away point.

Such an erratic start to the season could have blown Gazza's England chances, but Bobby Robson named him in the squad for the World Cup qualifying match against Sweden in Stockholm on 6 September. His inclusion, however, came with a price: like Venables, the England manager felt Gazza needed to grow up, and he said so publicly, with the warning that, if he didn't, Gazza could forget about playing for his country.

'Gazza's such a wonderful talent, that he's worth persevering with,' said Robson with commendable tolerance. 'He's coming through, but he must have the maturity to go with his skill.'

It says much for Gazza's likeable personality that two of his closest friends, Glenn Roeder and Chris Waddle, lent their support at what was arguably a crunch time in Gazza's international footballing life.

The former Newcastle captain made Gazza godfather to his baby son, William, and said, 'I have always spent a lot of time thinking of ways to help him mature and become more responsible, and making him godfather to my son is one of them.'

The next day – forty-eight hours before the Stockholm encounter – Chris Waddle, who had joined Marseilles for £4 million in the summer, made a personal plea, through the media, to his Geordie pal.

'This is the most important season of his career and, quite simply, he has got to respond,' said Waddle, who persuaded Gazza to join Spurs. 'People almost expect him to play the fool first and football second. He must turn that round – otherwise it will all go wrong for him . . . He owes it to himself, Terry Venables and to the club to give football everything . . . and walk away from trouble.'

It was the trouble, not the tomfoolery, that concerned and worried Robson. And although he used Gazza only as a sub for the injured Webb in the 0–0 draw in Sweden, he showed what long-term faith he had in the lad by launching what was tantamount to a battle campaign to beat his prodigy's on-field problems and give him a World Cup future.

In surely the first-ever talk-in over an individual, the England manager enlisted the help of Venables and all the senior England players to sort out the player he felt was 'daft as a brush'.

'We all have to work together on this one,' said Bobby. 'Gazza is learning and growing up, and it is a matter of how we can help him. It's very important for the boy to be rubbing shoulders with some of the players in the international side. They will bring him on and knock some of the silly things out of him. Terry and I have him for only three hours a day, while some players are with him for seven to eight hours.'

Naturally, Venables responded well to Robson's challenge, but in his own mind he felt Gazza was 'already most of the way there' to solving his temperament problems.

Paul was far from being nasty or bad-tempered, he said. And he put forward a view of Gazza that those teachers at Breckenbeds and Heathfield would have smiled at. 'Paul's like the naughtiest boy in class – a bit of a pest at times, but you can't help liking him. He wouldn't row with you or cause a bad atmosphere. He's more the sort who used to walk behind the teacher pulling faces. And if you tell him off, he's more sorry and apologetic than any other member of the team.'

While Venables agreed to continue to try to curb Gazza's on-field temper, he did feel the player was ready to play in the senior side. Robson, however, was far from convinced – not only about Gazza's temperament, but also about his defensive play – and when the team was announced for the World Cup qualifier in Poland the following month, Gazza was not in it.

The omission hit Gazza hard, particularly as Neil Webb was out of the team through injury, and Venables made it clear that his £2 million signing was playing the best football of his Tottenham career – 'including defending'.

Frustrated and hurt at the thought that he could not be trusted to play in such a crucial game, Gazza, uncharacteristically, poured out his feelings. All the time he had been in the England squad, he had been quiet and patient and had never put pressure on the manager to pick him. But now he felt he had to speak up.

'Last season I was perfectly happy to be part of the England squad, to get to know everybody, to listen and learn,' he said. 'I thought the idea was that, when the situation arose, I could be brought into the team with no worries about me having to adapt to the different demands of international football. But, from what I hear, I'm not going to get a chance because I can't be trusted. Well, if people think I'm going to let England down, I shouldn't be in the squad, full stop. It seems there is almost a campaign to keep me out of the team.'

On another day, Gazza the clown would have laughed at his pathetic paranoia. A campaign to keep him out? What a joke! Never in the field of football conflict had so much been done by so many to get him in the team!

In truth, Robson himself wanted Gazza to prove himself worthy of a full England cap. As he says today, 'Apart from Terry Venables, I saw more of Gazza in two years than any other manager in the country. And not only me. Dave Sexton, Don Howe, Mike Kelly saw him as well. We tailed Gazza more than any other England player *ever*. It was because he was so talented, yet so unpredictable. We had to keep checking that his talent was progressing the right way and his all-round game was improving; whether he was adopting a more defensive role, marking when he wasn't on the ball. I remember speaking to Terry Venables about his work capacity, too, and he would say to me, "You'd be surprised at Gazza – he's faster and trimmer than you think."

'And, in training with England, he was brilliant. He didn't just progress, he got better and better. He would go all out to be the best player, to show me he could do his stuff against the cream. He more than held his own against them. He was never not on song – he was always confident.'

So why, if he was playing well for his club and training brilliantly for his country, had Gazza not been given another chance in England's starting line-up? The answer, in a word, is trust. In Bryan Robson, McMahon and Webb, England had three reliable midfielders the manager knew he could trust. Quite simply, that did not apply to Gazza.

Trust was a word that would blow up in Robson's face before the end of the year.

In November 1989, with the World Cup just seven months away, England had two senior and B friendlies lined up – against Italy and Yugoslavia. Even with Webb still out,

Robson resisted the temptation to play Gazza in either game, preferring the permutation of several players – Platt, Hodge, Rocastle, McMahon, Phelan and Michael Thomas – to accompany Bryan Robson in midfield. But, significantly, Gazza was selected for the B match against Italy at Brighton, with four other youngsters – Dorigo, Paul Parker, Steve Bull, Gary Pallister – who were trying to break into the full England side.

On 14 November, more than 16,000 – the Goldstone ground's biggest crowd for three years – turned up for the match, no doubt encouraged by the morning's back-page headlines, one of which screamed, 'Don't blow a fuse, Gazza' – a reference to another warning from Dave Sexton to watch his temper.

The B team manager admitted that Gazza had the ability to get into any side in the world, but that was not enough at international level these days, he said.

And that dreaded word 'temperament' reared its fiery head again.

'Paul simply cannot afford to lose his cool,' said Sexton. 'He has listened and responded since he came into the Under-21 side and his fuse, which was very short, is now longer. But he must learn to walk away from trouble – an ability likely to be tested against the Italians.'

For Tony Dorigo, however, it was not Gazza's temper that worried him that night; it was the position the Spurs man had been told to play.

'As soon as I heard that Gazza was playing in front of me in left midfield, I thought: Oh, Christ, here we go – this is going to be tough.

'I was right. Two minutes after we kicked off, I never saw him again. I looked around early on to see if he was covering, and he'd gone on a run down the right wing. It panicked me a bit and I shouted at him to get back. But there was no point, because he always goes and does what he wants. And it's not always right to restrict him because, wherever he gets the ball, he can make things happen.

'He stayed wide on the right, so I had to call to other midfield players to shift across. Fortunately, the Italians were playing in such a way that we were not exploited. As it turned out, with Gazza not in front of me, I actually had more room to play and push forward against their right back. But, the truth is, we could have been jiggered that night.'

At the time, Dorigo admitted that with so many players trying to win World Cup places, the England squad had turned into 'a madhouse'. None, by all accounts, was madder than Gazza. But, that November night, he refused to be wound up by the cynical, shirt-tugging Italians; and, although he had a quiet game, his free-kick led to England's goal, giving them a 1–1 draw.

With the Italian job done, and no fuses blown, Gazza seemed on course for a smooth finish to what had been a rough, if exciting, calendar year. Sadly, it was the calm before the storm. Just one week later, at Selhurst Park, Gazza made what he admitted was the worst tackle of his life, and started an ugly punch-up involving eight Spurs and Crystal Palace players. What made it worse was that something he said to the referee, Joe Worrall, earned him his fifth yellow card of the season.

Still feeling bad about the clumsy challenge, Gazza went to the Palace boardroom after the match and told Palace manager Steve Coppell how sorry he was. Coppell thanked him and told him not to worry, because he had played well. But it was an unhappy Gazza who left South London that night: the brawl took the sheen off Spurs' 3–2 victory, which put them in sixth place in the League. And the booking meant that one more caution in November would result in an automatic three-match ban, ruling him out of any England game. With so much of his World Cup dream riding on selection, it was something Gazza hardly dared think about.

15

Millwall's ground, The Den, lies in a suburban backwater off the Old Kent Road, in a narrow street called Cold Blow Lane. Down the years the wind has blown bitterly indeed, but, for Gazza, on the evening of 12 December the air was warm with expectancy and hope.

After his blameless Brighton performance, he might have expected to return to the senior England squad, if not the team, for the Yugoslavia game at Wembley, where there was nothing but national pride at stake. But Bobby Robson had decided it was important for him to have a full game, not be on the fringe with the seniors. And that was good news for Gazza, particularly since Robson had, at last, decided to play him in the important central midfield position. Robson had decided that two days before. 'Right, let's find out about him,' he had said to Dave Sexton. 'Let's play him in the middle.'

The Press, of course, were cynical. Gazza was the people's choice for the World Cup, they pointed out, yet he still could not convince the man who mattered. Giving him a full game in the B team was merely sugaring the bitter pill.

Typically, Jimmy Greaves pulled no punches. He accused his former England team-mate of hiding Gazza in the B team when the kid should be showing what he could, or could not, do on the full international stage. All the B internationals did was give Robson an excuse to dither over his team selection, Jimmy said. And although Gazza had the flair and imagination to unlock defences 'unopened by England's predictable path towards goal', it would mean nothing, even if he played a blinder against the Yugoslavs.

Just what effect all the hullabaloo had on Gazza as he

walked on to the pitch that night is questionable. Certainly he knew it was a great test of character for him, for Sexton had given him the now customary warning that one moment of madness would ruin all the good work that had gone before. He was coming to the end of his probation and it was a crucial time for him.

Today, Sexton recalls: 'I think Paul was aware that the Italy and Yugoslavia games were vital if he was going to make it to the World Cup. Everyone who mattered to the England team selection was there – Robson, Howe and Kelly in the stand and me on the bench – and Paul was wise enough to realize it was a golden opportunity to prove he was good enough.

'Paul put on a marvellous, majestic midfield display. He was imaginative and excellent in all departments, and laid on a brilliant match-winning goal. He ran the game and, above all, was disciplined and in control. He proved he could be both brilliant and reliable.

'For me, that night, Paul staked a big claim for a first team place. He convinced a lot of people that he was going to make it – that he could live in international football, both physically and mentally. It was the best I'd seen him play – the first time I was convinced he could cope. I was delighted for him that it all came together because I knew how much he wanted to do well. It had been a question of time and maturity, and he confirmed my feelings – and, I think, Robson's – that he *could* do it. Without doubt, it was the turning point of Paul's England career.'

Robson, indeed, was pleased. 'Gazza looked great that night,' he recalls. 'Spurs had done a lot of work on him, teaching him all aspects of the game, and his weight had come down. He was talented on the ball, but played with a lot of responsibility, maturity and discipline. Yugoslavia were a good team and Gazza was probably man of the match. I think he may have been aware that it was a big match for him.'

It was a happy dressing room that night. The whole

team had played well and earned a good victory. Sexton went in and congratulated every player, singling no one out for special praise.

Robson, however, was impressed enough to go to the dressing room to have a word with Gazza.

'Dave was in charge of the team, but, as the boss, I wanted to put my bit in,' Robson remembers. 'I went up to Gazza as he was drying down after his bath and said something like, Well done, son, I was pleased you did this and that . . . you were good in this area, well done – some complimentary words.

' "Aye . . . aye, thanks, boss," was all I remember Gazza saying.'

After the post-match press conference, Sexton was walking to the car park when he bumped into Robson, who had parked his car next to his. They stopped and chatted briefly about the game.

'Bobby was pleased with the way it had gone,' says Sexton. 'The conversation turned to Gazza, and Bobby said he felt it was a very important game for the lad that night. I agreed, and we both said he'd been outstanding, had played majestically. We both felt that Gazza's performance had confirmed in our minds that he was now ready to be a reliable international.

'We didn't actually say it, but it was obvious we both knew we *now* had a player. And it was only a matter of when Gazza would be ready to be blooded in the first team.

'That chat, in the Millwall car park, was only brief. But it was a happy and positive one.'

For Gazza, the wind of Cold Blow Lane that cold December night seemed one of change.

The tubby little boy who had stolen the show in his 'Woolworths specials' all those years ago was, it seemed certain, about to step from the wings into the spotlight of the full international stage.

16

Astonishingly, it did not work out that way.

Bobby Robson stunned the press and the nation's sporting public, not to mention Gazza, by stating that, despite the majestic Millwall display, he still could not trust the lad to perform responsibly for England.

A bombshell, the newspapers called it. And, for once, the headline writers were right. After seven months in the shadows, Gazza had sprung from the senior subs' bench to play his heart out in what was arguably the most vital match of his life. He had performed in a way that had won him the praise of the man who controlled his World Cup destiny. He had been given the chance to show that he was good enough, mature enough, and he had grabbed it.

To read, now, that it all meant nothing, that his international career had progressed not an inch, was a kick in the teeth for Gazza.

I CAN'T TRUST GAZZA! – the huge type on the tabloid back pages screamed what to millions was a gross injustice.

But what did it mean?

Robson, the Press reported, said, 'The man who plays alongside Bryan Robson has to have a brain and discipline. He has to be able to work out when to go and when to stay, when to take chances. I'm not saying Gascoigne has not got a brain. But he still has to learn when to use it.'

Then, the football reporters claimed, Robson justified his comments by referring to England games several months before.

'Before Gazza's first match,' he said, 'I told him to play at outside right. He played on the *left*. Against Sweden, I put him on and told him to play in midfield. The first thing he did was to play in *front* of Gary Lineker. That's why I am saying to him, "I can't trust you yet, son," whatever the crowd say.'

The Millwall magic, as Jimmy Greaves had forecast, seemed to have counted for nothing. And the feeling – indeed, the fear – throughout the country that December was that Gazza's footballing virtuosity might never be appreciated at full England level. It had, sadly, happened before, with excitingly gifted flair players winning a fraction of the caps they were worth.

Gazza, it seemed then, was yet another victim of an England manager's distrust of maverick talent.

It was then that the press clamour for Gazza grew louder, with one mass-market tabloid organizing a phone-in, asking readers if they felt the Spurs star should be in the senior England team. Gazza polled twice as many votes as his main midfield rival, Steve McMahon. And readers' letters in response to Robson's distrust of Gazza prompted the headline: BRAINLESS GAZZA? NO, BOBBY'S BARMY.

At Spurs, Venables, having seen how Robson's snipe had affected Gazza, was stung into an uncharacteristic personal attack on the England manager.

'I trust Paul Gascoigne implicitly and if Bobby Robson doesn't, why is he still in the squad?' he said angrily. 'I find it all very strange . . . I can't understand why Robson constantly knocks him in public. Paul's a very sensitive lad underneath that larger-than-life exterior, and I think a lot of what Robson says hurts him.'

Venables, who admitted he had been disturbed for some time by Gazza's treatment at international level, felt that no other player in the team went out under the sort of pressure Gazza had. 'Every other game seems to be Gascoigne's last chance,' Venables said. 'He should be either in or out by now.'

Amid all the furore, Gazza kept a low profile, saying simply that, at just twenty-two, he needed encouraging, not knocking down. He admitted he had been hurt by criticism of his England performances, but stressed, defiantly, that he would continue to go out to try to do well and entertain.

The much-publicized saga infuriated Robson and, today, he insists that journalists were to blame for wrongly interpreting what he meant.

'I never said I couldn't trust Gazza,' he says passionately. 'That was the Press – headlines, that's all that was.

'We were playing a system with two wingers, which meant we had only two men in midfield. Those two main men have to be steady Eddies, totally reliable, to play the proper midfield role – not the loose midfield Gazza was playing.

'What I said was that I couldn't trust him yet to do the disciplined role, and the things you need to be a Bryan Robson, a Steve McMahon or a Neil Webb. He was not one of those players. I couldn't pick him to do that role.

'I used the word "trust", but it is how you interpret that word. And the Press need only one word. They can twist it and use the same word completely out of context. "I don't trust you, Gazza." Yeah, I said that. But not in the way they said it. I was angry with the Press on that. You can't take it up – you can't ring them up and say, "You twats, I didn't mean that and you know it. Why did you do it?" How can you?

'It wasn't a case of not trusting Gazza. I was simply saying he wasn't ready for that midfield role. There were some things in his game which had to mature.'

One way and another, it had been a controversial year, and it drew to an end with bizarre accusations that seemed to sum up the difficulties that go with the prestige of being a £2 million player.

First, Spurs received a letter of complaint from the Royal Mail, asking for an apology after Gazza kicked a 17-year-old Post Office cadet, Andrew Hicks, before that troubled Crystal Palace match. Andrew, dressed as the children's character Jess the Cat, was playing a joke game of soccer with Postman Pat and a bear, when Gazza jogged on to the Selhurst Park pitch. Andrew went up to him to shake hands, but Gazza, game for a laugh as usual, put a judo hold on the bear and gave the cat a friendly kick up the backside. Croydon District Head Postmaster John Berry, whose office is near Selhurst Park, demanded the apology because Andrew said the kick hurt. But Terry Venables laughed off the incident, saying Gazza did kick him, but only very lightly and in fun.

In the other accusation, Gazza was branded a yob by a former policeman, Derek Kitchin, who claimed the player deliberately kicked a ball into a TV cameraman's face, breaking his glasses, before a Littlewoods Cup tie against Tranmere Rovers. 'The poor bloke was in pain, but Gascoigne ran away smiling, without bothering to apologize,' said Mr Kitchin, who said he was reporting Gazza to Spurs and the FA. Granada TV, for whom the cameraman worked, took no action.

One wonders whether either incident would have come to light had Gazza not been in the spotlight as Britain's costliest footballer.

As if that was not enough, Gazza was then involved in another surprising row – this time over a book. He lent his name to a book of jokes and anecdotes, *Daft as a Brush*, but tried to dissociate himself from it after the publishers, Queen Anne Press, added an embarrassing reference to referees without Gazza's full knowledge. After settling his differences, Gazza told the publishers to give all his royalties to the BBC's Children in Need appeal. It was a generous gesture the cynics would have said he could well afford. For, in addition to the £100,000 Brooks boot deal earlier in the season, Gazza was expected to make another £100,000 from promoting his own range of boxer shorts.

If the newspapers were to be believed, the kid who could not afford his 10p subscription to Redheugh Boys' club was set to become Britain's richest footballer, as well as the costliest.

★

It took Gazza just eleven minutes of the first match of the New Year to put himself in the referee's notebook – and out of the game for six weeks. He cracked a bone in his left arm in a clash with Coventry's Lloyd McGrath at Highfield Road and returned to Tottenham with the arm in plaster. If that was a blow to a youngster with the approaching World Cup on his mind, it was disastrous for Spurs, who failed to win one of the seven games they were without him.

When he did return, early in February, it coincided with the news that Bryan Robson was out of England's match against Brazil on 28 March, following a groin operation. With World Cup places up for grabs, it provided a golden opportunity for Gazza to show Bobby Robson he was, indeed, to be trusted. And with the manager due to watch Spurs at Chelsea, Venables called for Gazza to be picked against the Brazilians – in Bryan Robson's role. 'People talk about Bryan's industry, but Paul covers as much ground as anyone in the Football League ... I won't accept any criticism of his work-rate,' Venables said.

The match at Stamford Bridge was tailor-made for Gazza to show off his skills and that much-desired maturity and self-control. But he blew it with a reckless retaliatory foul – what looked like a punch – on Chelsea's John Bumstead, right in front of the East Stand, where Robson was watching. Gazza was lucky not to be sent off, and the incident led, predictably, to yet another warning, interpreted in the press as: One more bust-up, Gazza, and you're out of the World Cup.

In Cairo to watch England's World Cup opponents Egypt, Robson said, 'What can you do? Of course, he's still in the reckoning, but I want to see no more of what he did at Chelsea. The boy still has to learn what he can do, what he can't do, and what is utterly impossible. Retaliation – he won't get away with it in the World Cup ... he just must learn not to bite.'

What must have been frustrating for Robson was that, as

with most Gazza fouls, there was no malice aforethought. Both Bumstead and the referee at Chelsea, George Tyson, agreed that Gazza was laughing and joking after the fracas, which earned him his eighth booking of the season.

'Gazza said sorry to me so many times I thought he was taking the mickey,' said Bumstead. 'I like him, but he's a strange lad.'

With four Wembley friendlies – against Brazil, Czechoslovakia, Denmark and Uruguay – lined up before England flew to Sardinia, the clamour for Gazza to be picked hotted up. And his confidence was given a boost when Graham Taylor, who would become the next England manager, said he was certain Gazza would be going to Italy.

'He is capable of doing things on a football pitch no one else can,' Taylor said. 'I know he doesn't always help himself, but I'm sure he will be in the World Cup squad.'

Former England star Ray Wilkins then joined the pro-Gazza band. He'd seen him at close quarters only once – during the Ibrox pre-season friendly when Wilkins was playing for Glasgow Rangers – but that was enough to appreciate that the cheeky Geordie was special. 'Gazza is clearly a lad with a short fuse,' said Wilkins, 'yet it's ridiculous to rule a player with his talent out of the World Cup reckoning.'

The fact remained, however, that in the second week of March Gazza had no idea if he would be in the team for the Brazil match later that month, let alone the World Cup squad.

And then, on the afternoon of 9 March, Robson went to a Football Writers' Association lunch in London. The next day, the whole country knew what Paul Gascoigne had to do to go to Italy.

It had, Robson announced, developed into a straight fight between Gazza and David Platt for one midfield place. They would be given one chance each to prove who was tops – Platt against Brazil on 28 March, and Gazza against Czechoslovakia on 25 April.

'I'd made up my mind in December to use these two matches, and others, against Denmark and Uruguay, to look at Gazza,' says Bobby. 'There was a fight for midfield places: Platt was coming good with Villa, Hodge was playing well with Forest, Rocastle quite well with Arsenal, McMahon was doing his stuff with Liverpool and Webb was nearer to fitness after his injury in Sweden. But there was still room for Gazza. I couldn't play him and Platt together, so they needed to have one match each to show me what they could do.

'By March, Villa were going so well I decided Platt should play against Brazil. It was a non-starter to put Gazza on as well; they were too young and inexperienced to play together against such formidable opposition, so I brought in McMahon in place of Robson or Webb.

'We won 1–0 in a tight, tense game. Platt and McMahon played very well. Platt's mileage and industry were superb and I thought, "Christ, he deserves to be playing again." But I had committed myself in the Press that Gazza would play against the Czechs. I had promised the boy he would get his chance.'

It is fair to say that, after the Brazil game, the odds were on Platt stealing that coveted midfield spot. Despite Gazza's unquestionable ability with a football, Robson had made it clear he was still not an all-round player who fitted his midfield requirements. And despite the loud and insistent Press clamour to take him to Italy come what may, it would not affect his judgement.

Robson's assistant, Don Howe, admits today that Platt would have got his vote. In those final months, he says, the two players were like horses galloping down the straight – and Platt was winning by a neck.

'Bobby would ask me to look at both players when Spurs and Villa played QPR,' says Don. 'He'd say, "I know you've got your job to do, but can you see how they're coming on for me?"

'They had such contrasting styles. Platt hadn't got the skills and grace, but was reliable and would get in the box, then get back in position. Gazza had all the flair and imagination, but would go missing. On League form, I was more impressed with Platt. Gazza didn't play too well against us, so I wasn't all that impressed.'

Even Gazza did himself no favours at that crucial time, Two weeks before Platt stepped out at Wembley to face the Brazilians, the gregarious Geordie admitted he started to panic when he was picked for England's squad. He blamed the extra pressure put on him, but said he could handle it if he was left alone to play his own game.

Dangerous words indeed for a hot-tempered player, whose predictable unpredictability had denied him more chances in the senior side. One of the reasons he was on the subs' bench, not the team, was that he had always seemed keener to play his own game than the manager's.

And then, amazingly, just one week before his own moment of World Cup truth, Gazza was given his *tenth* yellow card of the season, for fouling Millwall's Ian Dawes in Spurs' 1–0 win at the Den. Venables substituted his fiery star six minutes later.

It was as if Gazza had a death-wish; as if, deep down, he was looking for an excuse not to risk blowing the chance to fulfil his boyhood dreams. Bobby Robson, however, said nothing about the latest booking, and the Saturday before the Wednesday game against the Czechs, Gazza walked out to face Manchester United to a deafening roar from a packed White Hart Lane.

As a curtain-raiser for Gazza's big Wembley night, it was mouth-watering: two of Britain's most attractive sides, and the intriguing battle between England's midfield 'king', Bryan Robson, and the piquant pretender to his throne.

For Gazza, that afternoon was an opportunity to throw off all the irritations of a stuttering season and get himself in gear for the most crucial game of his international life; ninety minutes in which to show that he was good enough – and responsible enough – to grace the same Wembley pitch as the England manager's favourite son.

Gazza grabbed the chance with both hands and two magical feet, destroying United with an awesome display of arrogant skill, subtle passing and vision. It was a breathtaking show that had his Spurs manager smiling more broadly than ever.

'You will not see a better performance from any other midfield player, from any other club, in any other country,' Venables said. 'I have no doubts Paul can do what is asked of him at international level and we will all see on Wednesday night.'

The accolades heaped on Gazza after his North London extravaganza counted for nothing on Sunday night, when he reported at Burnham Beeches Moathouse, in Buckinghamshire, with the rest of the England squad. The United game was history. What was important to Gazza was the future – and his immediate future rested on a football match for his country on the famous turf of Wembley.

The audience would know that the maverick performer possessed the artistry to join the greats who had graced that stage.

But could he do it on the night – on his date with destiny?

17

It was after a team meeting the day before the match that Bobby Robson pulled his namesake to one side. 'You know what Gazza's like, Bryan,' he said. 'He's clever and likes to move around. But we can't have you going off looking for goals and have him going bloody everywhere as well. Lose the ball and they will come straight through us in midfield.

'Base your role off him. Give him his head, but support him. Let's see if he can show us what he can do.'

Bobby was confident in his skipper: he was an old head

and disciplined captain who could obey instructions. Normally he liked to attack, but on this night he would play behind Gazza and keep the ship steady while the lad did his clever things.

Bobby then told Gazza he could go out and do his stuff, comfortable in the thought that he had Robson behind him and Steven and Hodge out wide, providing a strong midfield.

During the two days' pre-match training, Gazza was more hyperactive than ever, and annoyed with the press for hyping up the game and the importance of him in particular.

Tony Dorigo remembers: 'The papers were running stories about the match nearly every day. One morning, over breakfast, Gazza picked up one paper and said, "I wonder what they're saying about me today." Sure enough, his name was all over the back page again. He was really wound up by all the attention. He said, "I can do without this. They want me to play well, but they keep piling on the pressure. It's ridiculous."'

Nerves make most players go quiet. But Gazza wanted to be on the go, and talk, more.

As Don Howe says, 'He'd be twisting and turning and walking round. He'd go over there and have a chat with one player, then on to somewhere else. He has a natural enthusiasm to play football; he loved it *all* the time. After training and after lunch, most of the players would enjoy a rest, but Paul would be out on the five-a-side pitches with young kids.

'The kids would turn up to get autographs and they would be knocking a ball around outside, and Paul would go out and join them. He did it quite naturally and would be doing all his tricks and joking around.

'For him, that was relaxing. There were times when Bobby or I would have to tell him to stop and rest his legs. He would do it without any complaint, but most of the time we let him get on with it because he was the type of person who likes to be busy and active. If you try to keep a naturally active person still, you're going against their natural characteristics. Gazza is very similar to Kevin Keegan, who also liked to be busy – he wasn't as hyperactive as Gazza, though.

'Even on the coach to Wembley, Gazza couldn't sit still. He stood up the whole way – the whole twenty miles! – playing cards. There'd be four or five of them playing round a table and Gazza would be the one standing in the aisle. Bobby would turn round and say, "Hey, you're playing football tonight – *sit down!*" Gazza would sit down quickly, but, a few minutes later, he'd be up again. He finds it impossible to sit down quietly and relax.'

Before a match, Gazza normally laughs and jokes around, but in the Wembley dressing room that night, he was edgy.

'He was still lively, but you could tell he wasn't quite the same,' Dorigo recalls. 'He was a little bit quieter than normal, and when a minute goes by and you don't hear from Gazza, you know there's something wrong.

'He was nervous and tense, and sweating up through the stress of it. I noticed his face getting redder than usual and his twitches were more evident that day, too. I don't know any player who had so much expected of him as Gazza had for that game.

'All the players were aware of the focus on him and were concerned for him. I felt for him, too, and was worried up to a point. I'd come through the Under-21s and the full England team at more or less the same time and it wasn't nice to see all that pressure on him that night.

'I never said anything in particular to him before a game, but, before we left the dressing room, I went up to him and said, "Just go out there and do your stuff, Gazza – you show 'em." He appreciated that. He said "Ta very much," and sort of gritted his teeth and clenched a fist, as if to say, "Yeah, that's what I'm going to do."

'He wanted to do so well, and was so hyped up, that when the ref blew up a couple of times early on, Gazza got all uptight and disputed the decisions. I feared he was going to fly off the handle and get booked, but, thankfully, he calmed down and started to play brilliantly.'

The Czechs went ahead after eleven minutes through a Skuhravy header, but Steve Bull ran on to a delightful through ball from Gazza to equalize six minutes later. On twenty-four minutes Butcher nodded back a Gazza near-post corner for Pearce to score his first England goal. Ten minutes into the second half, Gazza dribbled past two Czechs on the right and pulled the ball back from the byline for Bull to score his second. With ten minutes left, Kubik scored from a free kick to put some pressure on England, but then Gazza sewed the game up with a brilliant solo effort from a Dorigo pass.

Those are the bald goal statistics that state England won 4-2. What they do not state is that in terms of sheer crowd-thrilling magnificence, Paul Gascoigne had the game of his young life. He took the free kicks, and the corners. He made telling passes and went on dribbling runs. He scored a goal and created the others. He ran the show; ran it with a sublime arrogance that revived memories of the wizardry of Mister Puskas and his magical Magyars.

Gazza will never forget the game. And neither will Bobby Robson.

'It was very fulfilling to see Gazza have such a good game,' he says today. 'I was so pleased for him. He excited the crowd and sent them home laughing with a fantastic solo goal. The Czechs came back to 3-2 and it tightened the game up. With minutes to go, Gazza was on his heels. He had done so much running his stockings were over his shins and he was really leggy.

'He was so physically gone I wanted to bring him off. I said to myself, "He's done enough – I've seen enough to know he's good. I'm not interested in the last few minutes because what he had done for the last eighty-odd was superb. I'll take him off and protect the result."

'I was just thinking about that when Wright made an

attack and squared a ball to Dorigo and, out of the blue, this kid Gascoigne found some energy from somewhere. He saw the move and went through the midfield – about forty yards – to get on this pass from Dorigo. He went past a player and as the keeper came out, Gazza blasted a left-foot shot into the roof of the net.

'Had I taken him off, nobody would have seen that goal, and I didn't think he had the energy to do it. But he proved me wrong. His energy level was really very good.

'In the dressing room afterwards, Gazza was really on top. The kid knew he had played well and was very pleased with his performance. I went over to him and said, "Well done Gazza – that was super stuff, son. You were bloody great. You were involved in three of the goals. Good lad."

'And Gazza said, "Fouwa" – four in heavy Geordie. I said, "What do you mean, four?"

'"The second was off my corner," he said.

'I said, "Hey, any bugger can take a corner."

'Gazza just laughed. "Yeah, but not the way I can take them, and it was me who took that one."

'That's Gazza all over. So, I conceded – a bit reluctantly, mind – that he did have a hand in all the goals.

'I could tell he was very proud that I was pleased with his performance. He had that huge smile of his all over his face. It clearly meant a lot to him to hear it from me.

'But I knew I couldn't judge him completely on that game alone – you can't with any player. He had thrilled everyone and we were all pleased. I was talking with Don Howe later and said, "Right, we'll have to see if he can do it again. We won't leave him out – we'll pick him again against different opposition and see if he can do it again." That's the only way to be sure it wasn't a one-off that went all his way.

'We beat Denmark and Gazza did well again. He worked hard, got back, tackled and won the ball. I'd tell him, "You're doing well, son, I'm keeping you in the team." He was loving it. He's a big match player – he can't wait for them to come. He knows he can do it.

'He was going so well, I knew he had a real chance of getting in the team – let alone the squad – for Italy.'

On Tuesday 21 May, all twenty-six members of the England squad sat on the lawn at Burnham Beeches Moathouse, waiting for Bobby Robson to read out the names of the twenty-two players he would be taking to Italy. The four who were not going had been told, but the others did not know that.

'It was a bit like getting your exam results,' Tony Dorigo says. 'So it was a relief to get the final confirmation.

'I think that Gazza knew, deep down, that he would be picked, but it's hard to know for sure what he's thinking, because he's always the same – always 100 per cent nutcase, running around doing stupid things.'

If his cheeky confidence is anything to go by, Gazza *would* have felt he had done enough to clinch a seat on the plane. After all, hadn't he told Robson himself: 'Once you put me in the team, I'll be there to stay'?

18

In Sardinia, Gazza was like a kid in a toy shop. There were so many attractions, he didn't know where to start. During the day, he always wanted to be doing something and found it impossible to sit still. At night, he didn't want to sleep, and Bobby Robson says he almost had to lock the bedroom door on him.

'He was always on the go,' Bobby says. 'You can't sedate him. I had to make sure he was in bed and going to sleep, otherwise he'd be walking down the corridor to someone else's room and talking to them until one or two in the morning.

'I'd have to tell him, "Stay in your room. Everyone's

tired. It's been a hot day. Everyone's trained hard and we've got a big match coming up in a couple of days. You may not be able to sleep, but others can. Stay out of their bedrooms!"

'But he wasn't a headache. You've got to take him for what he is – hyperactive. You'd be chatting to him and some of the lads, then get up to go. You'd walk through to another part of the hotel and look round, and Gazza would be on your shoulder. You'd think, "Hang on, I've just left you in another room – where did you come from?" He was just everywhere.

'He's a lovable kid – there's no doubt about how lovable he is. I have a great deal of affection for him and have never had a bad time with him. He's always laughing and seeing the funny side of things – and I don't know anyone who doesn't like him.'

It was this happy outlook on life that endeared Gazza to everyone he met in Italy – hotel receptionists, waiters, chambermaids, even security guards.

'Gazza has that way with him,' says Don Howe. 'He has that smile and would always be chatting to people. He got to know all the security guards. We'd have to go past them at least twice a day and Gazza would always stop and have a chat with them. He couldn't speak Italian, but he has no shyness and would converse in a jokey way they would understand. He just came across as a friendly person. If he went for a walk round the hotel, you'd always see him laughing and joking with young soldiers who were also guarding the hotel. He is the type of lad who gets on with everyone, and everyone where we stayed knew Gazza. They just reacted to his smile.

'All this was before he started to play. And, of course, as the tournament went on, he became a celebrity in his own right. The hotel staff could see that he had the same fun-loving personality on the football pitch. He took every game by the scruff of the neck, and he did so well that people who didn't know who he was before the World Cup sat up and said, "Who's that?"'

From the moment he arrived in Italy, Gazza was determined to have a great time, particularly when the football was over for the day and he and the rest of the party relaxed on the beach. In Sardinia there was an aqua-centre, and Gazza would be there nearly every day, with a big grin, saying, 'What have you got for me today?' He was the first to get a snorkel and a pair of flippers, then a pedalo, then a windsurfing board.

'He wanted to have a go at everything,' says Tony Dorigo. 'And he's got so much nervous energy, he can't sit still for five minutes.

'On the beach, everyone was taking it easy one day when Gazza got hold of a load of miniature soccer balls and persuaded some of the lads to throw them at him while he was in the sea. He was diving all over the place, heading and throwing them back at the lads – and at other people he didn't know, who were minding their own business.

'My wife bought a huge bag of crisps one day. When she wasn't looking, Gazza crunched them up into little crumbs, then ran off. He took a pedalo out to sea and tied it to a buoy, so that he could sunbathe. My wife discovered he was the crisp culprit and rounded up other wives to pedal out and splash him. Far from being annoyed, Gazza loved it and turned it into a game of pirates by chasing them and crashing into their pedalo, while humming the theme from "Jaws". It was always anything for a laugh.'

Not all his antics raised the desired giggle, however. Mike Kelly remembers one incident when he watched Gazza in the sea near a lot of rocks.

'He was always trying to find something to do when we weren't training,' says Mike. 'One day, I was sitting on the patio outside my hotel room watching him trying to get on a wind-surfing board. He kept falling off, but the more he failed to get on, the harder he tried. I was worried because I could see rocks near where he kept falling off. In the end, I couldn't stand it any longer and went down and said, "Knock it on the head, Gazza, you're going to get injured."

'He was as good as gold and said, "All right," and dragged the board back on the beach.'

In Sardinia, there is a very smart golf course, which extended an invitation to the England squad to play a round free of charge. Unfortunately, Gazza proved more of a handicap for Bobby Robson than the course. Club rules stated that golfers must wear shirts, but Gazza didn't think that applied to him. Worse, he insisted on having a buggy of his own and treated it like a dodgem car, zig-zagging up the fairways, bumping into team-mates' carts and generally disturbing the tranquillity of the course. Not surprisingly, Robson got complaints about his eccentric golfer, and had a word with him back at the hotel.

Tony Dorigo is the best golfer in the England squad, with a handicap of eight. He was favourite to win a golf competition – until he was drawn to go round with Gazza and Waddle.

'All the lads laughed,' says Tony. 'But I went up to Gazza and said, "Now, come on, don't muck about. If we're serious we could play well. I'll give you a few tips and one of us might win."

'Gazza can play a bit, too, and he said, "Yeah, okay then, Tony."

'I felt sure he would drive me potty, but he didn't play up, and he listened when I gave tips. He played well that day and the only time he messed around was when the BBC TV cameras were around. We all teed off – then he and Waddle suddenly started doing a dance on the tee wiggling their bums at the camera and singing. I thought, "Oh, my God, here we go." But they were fine the whole way round and didn't put me off at all.

'Gazza and I got through to the top six in the play-offs, and eventually I lost to Steve McMahon in the final.'

Gazza knew from their Under-21 days that Dorigo was pretty useful at table tennis, too, and would want to play all the time – even when Tony just wanted to sunbathe.

'In the first hotel there was a table tennis table in the basement and, of course, Gazza was the first to find it,' says Tony. 'We went down there and ended up playing eleven games. Gazza is very competitive and was intent on winning. But you have to watch him. If you didn't mention the score for a while, then asked what it was, you could guarantee he would be winning by a few points. He must have done me once or twice, but if you caught him he would just start laughing.

'Normal table tennis wasn't good enough for Gazza – he always liked to try something different. Would you believe, he developed a double-handed back-hand shot – as in outdoor tennis!

'I won our tough match 6–5 and Gazza didn't like it too much. He wasn't a bad loser at all, but he threw the bat down and said, "You bugger – I'll get you next time."

'I enjoyed table tennis, but Gazza liked to play *all* the time. Sometimes I would have to say, "No, leave me alone." But a lot of the time he would get me playing when I didn't particularly want to. He has that way of getting you going.'

The team tried to get Gazza himself going when they gave him a belated birthday party in Sardinia. Bobby Robson presented him with a cake and everyone tried to put him on the spot by shouting, 'Speech . . . speech.'

Unfazed, Gazza jumped up and brought the house down by sending himself up in a hilarious off-the-cuff speech.

'I was great at seven,' he said. 'At seventeen I went to Newcastle and showed 'em all how to play . . . they offered me a grand a week and I said I'm not going to take a drop for you . . . at twenty I was the greatest player in the league . . . at twenty-one I was earning £7,000 a week . . .' And so it went on. It was Gazza at his most appealing, and he got a standing ovation.

The Italian heat affected all the players differently, but Gazza found it more difficult to adapt than most.

'At home, he would normally never run out of energy, but in that first week, he was struggling for breath,' says Dorigo. 'Once he got acclimatized, though, he was running around like a loony, as usual.

'Players not taking any part in one of the matches are called "nuggets", and it was customary for them to kick a ball around in the warm-up gyms in the stadiums while the rest of the squad were getting changed. The gyms have artificial grass, which took a stud, and Gazza would get kitted up and come up to the gym for a kickabout, rather than sit in the dressing room, stretching or whatever. He wasn't worried in the least about saving his legs. He was more relaxed kicking around than being in the dressing room, because he gets restless.'

The worrying fear that Gazza could lose England a match as well as win it was exemplified in the final warm-up fixture against Tunisia on 2 June. He miscued a diagonal back pass to Steven and gave the ball to Hergal who, astonishingly, volleyed it over Shilton's head from about forty yards. The Tunisians had not played together since failing to qualify for the World Cup six months earlier, but they came close to embarrassing England. It took a Steve Bull header eleven minutes from the end to spare their blushes.

If this costly slip knocked Gazza's confidence, he did not show it. He was picked for the first match, against Ireland in Cagliari, and could not wait to get on the pitch, despite the lightning flashing around the Sant' Ella stadium. He was psyching himself up and doing his best to get his team-mates going, too.

As Robson says, 'The Robsons and Shiltons are confident in a calm, mature way, but Gazza has such a confidence in his own ability that he firmly believes he's going to be the matchwinner, jack-the-lad and master of the pack, every time he plays. One or two players got apprehensive and I was worried for them. But I wasn't worried for Gazza. Nothing ever frightens him. He was sky high with confidence and couldn't wait to get on the pitch.

'That Ireland game didn't suit him at all, because it was raining and windy and the ball was in the air a lot. And it was a real rough and tumble in which we had to fight for everything. Gazza showed a character that he had not been asked to show before: he chased people, got in tackles, scrambled. He scrapped. And I was pleased with him. I had to pick him to play in the next game against Holland.'

Despite the goalless scoreline, England's performance – particularly Gazza's – against the reigning European champions gave cause for genuine optimism, and Bobby Robson's team went into the game against Egypt with a realistic chance of topping Group F. That they did was due to a Gazza free-kick, cheekily placed in the wrong spot, which Mark Wright headed home. The goal gave England the only win in their group, and the right to meet Belgium in Bologna in the first round of the knockouts.

If the team were now brimming with confidence, Gazza was positively buzzing with it and enjoying the media attention his brilliant play was attracting.

'People thought it might be a pressure, but he revelled in it,' says Dorigo. 'Not that Gazza was the type to sit down and talk about the adulation. He doesn't sit down and talk seriously about anything really. The only times I've seen him in a serious mood were when I was rooming with him and he was talking about a girl he really liked, and before the Czech game when the pressure was bothering him.

'Everyone knew he was playing fantastically, but he's not the sort of guy you can go up to and say, "You're playing great, Gazza," because he's likely to make some wisecrack, because he'll think you're taking the mickey.

'As the tournament went on, and the better he played, the more he emerged and grew up.'

Robson, too, noticed the new-found discipline and maturity – off the field as well as on it. If Gazza had put on a few pounds, for example, he would ask the team doctor's permission not to go to the dining room for lunch or dinner.

'He'd learned a lot over the years, especially about his weight,' says Robson. 'He knew that if he came down and saw the food, he would be tempted to eat it. I was extremely pleased with that very good self-discipline.

'He was showing it against tough-tackling opponents, too. Virtually every day, Don and I had drilled it into him not to react to players who wound him up, hoping to get him sent off. I talked to the players en bloc, but I would pull Gazza aside after team talks and say, "You know what I've just said – well, it really applies to you . . ." He always took it well. He'd say, "I know, I know . . . I won't let you down."

'He didn't. And he had cut out chatting to referees, too. As the World Cup went on, I found myself putting more and more faith in him.'

The prospects of England's surge continued looking good in Bologna that night of 26 June, when Gazza lofted a free-kick deep into the Belgian box and Platt hooked in the winner minutes from time. For the next opponents were Cameroon, who, despite topping their group and beating Colombia in the second phase, did not look capable of stopping England reaching their first World Cup semi-final for twenty-four years.

On a night of high drama in Naples, however, Gazza the hero became the villain, as he fouled Cameroon sub Milla in the box and allowed the African side back in the game with a penalty. They went ahead four minutes later, but two penalties from Gary Lineker – one seven minutes from the end of ninety minutes, the other in extra time – took England on to Turin to meet West Germany.

With the prize a place in the World Cup Final, the stage was set for an epic, nail-biting thriller.

And Gazza, the kid the manager had not trusted, the midfielder with the talent but not necessarily the temperament for the big time, could not wait to get his boots on.

He had dreamed of entertaining the people who stood on the terraces at St James's Park. Now, at just twenty-three, he was to perform in front of a world audience, 30 million of them TV viewers in England.

It did not frighten him one bit.

If ever a game needed Gazza's mature, more disciplined attitude, it was that sultry July night in Turin. With one caution already against his name, he needed only one more to rule himself out of the final, should England beat the Germans.

He knew it. Bobby Robson and the team knew it. And the thousands of England supporters in Italy and at home knew it.

Throughout the first half and fourteen minutes of the second, England matched the Germans in everything. The defence, with Butcher as sweeper, snuffed out the much-feared German strike-force of Voller and Klinsmann; the midfield, with Gazza irrepressibly rampant, battled to manacle Matthäus; Lineker and Beardsley, up front, ran their hearts out, probing for a breakthrough.

And then a Brehme free-kick, deflected by Parker, looped crazily over the back-pedalling Shilton to put the Germans 1–0 ahead.

For English fans, the World Cup dream began to fade.

Ten minutes from time, however, slack German defending let in Lineker, who drilled in an equalizer to take an exciting tie breathtakingly into extra-time. English supporters in the stadium, and millions more in armchairs at home, breathed more easily. England were back in it, and the way they were playing anything was possible.

The football skill was there. So was the fight. The dream came back. Maybe, as Robson had ventured, England's name was on the cup.

In the 100th minute of heart-stopping confrontation, a German picked up the ball on his right touchline, in front of the team benches. Gazza, pumped up and in full battle cry, crunched in hard but fair, his eyes on the ball. The German went down, in supposed pain. The German bench went up as one in anger. And the Brazilian referee blew his whistle and walked towards the touchline.

Gazza helped his fallen opponent to his feet. Then he turned to the referee, with an apologetic smile, but a worried look, too, betraying his fear. Slowly, agonizingly slowly, the referee reached inside his shirt and then brought out a yellow card.

He showed it to Gazza. Then, with an authoritative stiff-armed movement, he held it high and showed it to the crowd.

Gazza looked at the referee with a sort of hopelessness. He looked at his manager, despairingly. And then his lip began to tremble and his eyes filled and he began to cry.

For Paul Gascoigne, that was the moment his own World Cup dream ended; the moment he knew that, if victory came that night and took England to Rome for the final, he would not be playing in it.

Bobby Robson wanted to jump on the referee.

'I was clenching my fists and my stomach was churning over,' he says. 'That's when being a manager is tough, because you have to keep some sort of decorum and look quite sane about things when you're really going mad.

'I thought, Christ, if we go through, Gazza won't be able to play, and he deserves to play more than any player I know. He'd done as much, if not more, than any player in the squad to get us there. He did so much for us. He did special things for the team. He did things for us he hadn't done so well for Tottenham. His mileage was unbelievable. He'd become an integral part of the team.

'For that kid not to have played in the World Cup Final would have been the tragedy of football, you know. The tragedy of football.

'The second he saw that yellow card, Paul registered instantly what it meant. His eyes were glazed; he was distraught.

'Gary Lineker read the situation immediately. He knows

Gazza well and knew what might happen. He gestured and called to the bench. "Have a word with him," he said. "Keep your eyes on him . . . he can go."

'It was nice of Lineker to tell me. But I thought, What the hell can I do? I, too, felt Gazza might go berserk and do something daft and get sent off, but I was on the bench, not the pitch. So I yelled back, "*You* look after him. *You* slow him down. *You* keep hold of him and make sure he doesn't do anything daft.'

Gazza's head did drop; and for two, maybe three, minutes, he ran around that Turin stadium in a daze, not knowing what was going on. For those minutes, the discipline he'd worked so hard to get right deserted him: he was out of position, out of touch, out of his mind. He was wandering around, ragged and aimless, tears streaming down his face, his mind not on the match but on the caution that had killed his dream. He had, indeed, 'gone', but not in the way Lineker feared. Gazza in those miserable minutes had 'gone' in terms of the most potent, most deeply wounding, crushing disappointment.

And then, quite dramatically and thrillingly for all those who were watching him, he snapped out of it.

Suddenly his head cleared. His mind came back to the game. His legs took him where his team needed him to be.

His dream was over. But not England's. They could still win this game, still get to the final. Gazza gritted his teeth and got back in the battle. He was running for himself, for his team-mates, for his family, for his country.

And when the referee, who had broken Gazza's heart, blew his whistle and called an end to 120 minutes of pulsating football, Gazza stood in the middle of the field, a little lost, not quite sure what happened next.

He looked towards the England bench and Bobby Robson, the man who had needed so much convincing that he was good enough, mature enough.

And the tears began to flow again.

*

The stalemate was to be resolved, unsatisfactorily, with the dreaded penalty shoot-out. Robson walked out on the pitch and made for Gazza, who was not one of England's five nominated spot-kickers; in the event of a tie after five penalties, the manager wanted him to take the sixth. But Gazza was still crying and almost inconsolable.

'I put my arm round him, fighting to keep away my own tears,' Robson recalls. 'I felt so sorry for him. It was so emotional out there on the pitch, feeling what he was feeling. I thought, "Poor little bugger." He'd played so well, ran his heart out.

'My eyes filling up, I said, "You can't play in the final, Paul. But what you *can* do is to make sure everyone else can, son. You've done great to get us here. Now, see it out. Do it for us.'

'I kept saying these things, and Paul, hardly able to look at me through his tears said, "Don't worry . . . don't worry about me. Trust me. I'll do it."'

As it turned out, Gazza did not have to take that sixth penalty. Pearce, then Waddle, missed from the spot and the West Germans won the shoot-out 4–3.

The subs on the England bench thought it funny when they saw Gazza crying. They were so keyed up, they laughed out loud to relieve their tension. 'Dave Beasant was the first to spot Gazza crying and told us to keep our eyes on him,' says Tony Dorigo. 'Sure enough, his face was all serious, as he fought to get the ball, but then he would suddenly stop and start crying again. It was like an on and off switch.

'He was running around, trying to tackle and close players down. Once, he sprinted at Matthäus and we thought he was going to tackle him, but Matthäus dropped his shoulder and passed him. Gazza stood there, his face scrunched up, and he started crying again. At that point, all the boys were looking at each other laughing. Gazza would compose himself and try another tackle and when he missed that he would cry again. And we would laugh.

'After the game, we all felt so sorry for him and weren't laughing. I was one of the first to go over to him. His face was bright red and his eyes were bloodshot. His face was wet with tears and sweat. I put my arm round him and he buried his head in my shoulder. He was crying his eyes out – I could hear him sobbing.

'I said to him, "You were magnificent." Then Terry Butcher came over to him and Gazza got his head up and waved to the crowd, tears still streaming down his face.'

The dressing room was not a good place to be.

All the players had their heads down and were taking a long time to get their boots and kit off. Robson came in and didn't know what to say, but told them no team deserved to lose like that, and they had restored England's football reputation and put it on the pedestal where it belonged. But nobody lifted their heads; they just sat there, trying to take it in that they had lost the most important game of football for England in twenty-four years. Gazza was still crying, but Robson's most vivid memory of that sad room is looking at Peter Shilton and the dejection in his face that said, 'I'm forty and I am going to retire, and I could have finished as a World Cup winner.'

The same sad quietness filled the coach on the way back to the hotel. Then, unexpectedly, someone – probably Waddle or McMahon – started singing. Gazza sat there for a moment, inactive for once, still lost in thoughts of what might have been; then he picked himself up and started joining in the usual raucous team favourites. Within a few minutes he had taken over, laughing and joking and taking the mickey, his court-jester's hat back in place.

The humour was still there, three days later, in Bari, when England met Italy for the third place spot. Tony Dorigo, playing in his full debut, will never forget it. Hearing a loud cheer from the subs' bench half-way through the first half, he looked round to see Gazza and Terry Butcher leading a mini 'Mexican wave'. For the rest of the half, he could see them out of the corner of his eye and hear Gazza singing and yelling 'Weeeee!' as the subs jumped up and down.

For the football-crazy boy from Gateshead, the World Cup was ending on a high, with a big smile where the tears had been.

If he thought his special brand of soccer fun had made an impact on the Italians, it was nothing to what was waiting for him back home.

19

He went away a footballer not sure of a place in the team, and returned a hero with a place in the hearts of the nation.

There were more than twenty others in the England squad, but it was Gazza that the multitude wanted to see when the players flew in to Luton Airport from Italy on Sunday 8 July. It was 'Gazza . . . Gazza' they were yelling as the brass band played *Rule Britannia* and *Land of Hope and Glory*, and the team climbed up on to an open-top, double-decker bus and rode in triumph through the screaming streets of the Bedfordshire town.

They came out of homes and offices and factories and pubs, more than 200,000 of them, to applaud the boy who had not been ashamed to let the world see how much football meant to him; who, with adventurous, colourful play and an infectious, audacious cheek, had brightened a game that had been drab for too long.

That Sunday afternoon, the tears of Turin had been wiped away in the joy of being part of England's best-ever performance on foreign soil; and, once he had got over the shock at the hugeness of the homecoming welcome, Gazza basked in the warmth of it.

It was, of course, not enough for him to just stand there, in open-neck shirt, acknowledging the cheers with a dignified wave. Outrageous and full of energy as ever, Gazza put on a pair of giant plastic boobs and joke hats and kept going from side to side of the bus, repaying every scream, every cheer, from the yelling masses with a laugh, and planting wet kisses on the faces of his smiling team-mates.

It was a parade of passion, an uninhibited, overwhelming display of national pride, and the kid who yearned to play in the 'big team' all those years ago, revelled in the nerve-tingling sensation of being the cause of it.

For Gazza the returning hero, that afternoon and the emotional welcome that awaited him in Dunston made it a Sunday to savour – a day to end all days.

But it was only the beginning.

For the next two months, the country found itself in the grip of what the newspapers came to call Gazzamania. Gazza's face was in the newspapers every day, on the back sports pages but also – when his girlfriend walked out – on the front pages, too.

It was an astonishing hype of a sports personality, the likes of which had never been seen before. One got the feeling Gazza had only to blow his nose to make a headline. On Spurs' pre-season tour of Norway, he made the trip worthwhile for the reporters by getting booked and substituted within half an hour of the first match.

Predictably, Bobby Robson was asked to comment on this aberration, and made the emotive plea to Gazza 'not to be stupid and throw it all away', which made headlines again.

Five days later, in his first match in Britain – a friendly against Hearts – Gazza was booked again, after just twelve minutes this time. That should have been the end of it. But Gazza told the national newspaper that had him under contract that the ref had booked him for smiling, and the Scottish FA reported him to the English FA for what they considered unfair criticism. Gazzamania was gaining momentum. Then Gordon Taylor, the players' union boss, stoked it up with an eve-of-new-season plea to referees and players to treat Gazza fairly to save him being driven out of the game like George Best.

The crowd, not to mention the reporters and photographers, wanted a goal from Gazza in the first appearance at White Hart Lane since the World Cup. And Gazza did not let them down, blasting one of Spurs' goals in the 4–1 win over West Ham in Ray Clemence's testimonial.

The Football League then acknowledged Gazza's pulling power by breaking with tradition and deciding to screen the Tottenham–Manchester City match to 300 million viewers in sixty countries instead of the match involving last season's champions, Liverpool. And the *Radio Times* used his photograph on the front cover to publicize his appearance on BBC's new Radio Five station.

Hungry for any story where they could use 'Gazza' in big headline type, one tabloid claimed an exclusive by revealing a unique clause in the player's Spurs contract, guaranteeing him 50 per cent of any fee over £2 million, should the club transfer him. Not to be outdone in a big-money story, a rival paper revealed, also exclusively, that Spurs had turned down £5 million bids for Gazza from Italian clubs AC Milan, Fiorentina and Genoa.

Gazzamania was growing bigger by the day. And the season had not even begun.

In the week before the big kick-off, the pace quickened. Gazza, the public were informed, was going to be a millionaire: business deals involving a video, a record, advertising, a computer game, a poster magazine, plus his personal appearances and exclusive newspaper contract would boost his off-the-field earning power and put him on a financial par with the world's top golfers and racing drivers.

Not surprisingly, the money-men advising the world's hottest footballing property decided it would be sensible to try to protect Gazza from merchandizing rip-offs by registering his nickname as a trademark. That it was all getting slightly out of hand was evident in a candid admission from Gazza that the outside pressures were so fierce he sometimes felt like 'doing a runner'. The only place he felt safe, he said, was on the pitch. Prophetically, he said, he feared things might get worse.

But, in the rush to capitalize on the phenomenon that was Gazza, no one was listening. And even if they were, no one could hear for the deafening sound of money talking.

It was almost a relief to get to the first Saturday of the season. Gazza took the 'carry on clowning' advice of referees' secretary Duncan Jackson to heart, and thrilled a Tottenham full house with his cheeky personality and a goal in the 3–1 win over Manchester City.

'A breath of fresh air for football' was how Kevin Keegan described him the next day. But the former Newcastle favourite feared for him in the light of the media's staggering and ludicrous Gazza overkill, and added an ominous warning: 'He could finish on skid row or be top of the pile in ten years.'

Gazzamania was speeding relentlessly on. And danger signs that it would have to be stopped loomed large two days after that opening game, when Gazza confessed he hid in a car boot to escape the fans outside the ground.

The next day Terry Venables added to the hype, stating – happily for Spurs fans – that Gazza was 'one player money can't buy' and that the superstar wasn't going anywhere.

Where he *was* going, sadly, was round the twist!

He was young and fit and healthy. But, alas, the personal appearances, the never-ending glare of the media spotlight, and the mental strain of being the country's costliest, wealthiest, most gifted, most entertaining, most controversial sportsman were getting to him, draining him, giving him literally sleepless nights.

He was, he confessed candidly, becoming frightened of

the consequences of Gazzamania and where it was going to end.

On Monday 3 September, he knew.

After Gazza arrived for the match at Arsenal at the weekend, complaining of feeling tired, Venables decided enough was enough: if off-the-field interests were affecting Gazza's performances on it, they would have to stop. It was a decision made by an experienced man of the world, who not only cared about the boy but, more importantly, knew and appreciated what he was going through and what dangers he could face.

Within twenty-four hours, Gazza's business advisers cancelled six personal appearances and announced they would not be taking on any more. And that Monday evening, Britain's most likeable, if pressurized, Geordie, went on the *Wogan* show and confirmed that the brakes had been put on the Great Gazza Roadshow.

After fifty-seven days of quite extraordinary headline-making hype, Gazzamania, he hoped, was over.

Gazza is, they keep reminding us, the greatest footballing phenomenon since George Best, who was supposedly driven out of the game and destroyed by the media's morbid fascination for stripping bare the innermost secrets of heroes they have created. Not surprisingly, the knockers, the doom-watchers with an insatiable appetite for negative thinking, have been predicting that Gazza will go the same way; that he will fall victim to the evil temptations lurking amid the bright lights of the capital and in the minds of the dubiously motivated people living there.

They are people who do not know the lad. Those who do – those caring and compassionate Geordies who have seen him grow up, watched him cultivate and nurture his rich, rare talent, admired his dedication in his quest for excellence, enjoyed his sense of fun, and perhaps been victims of it – will laugh at the thought of Gazza changing into a media-created monster, hell-bent on self-destruction.

At a critical and vulnerable time of his life, when his dreams of entertaining the people on the terraces were being crushed under the weight of Colin Suggett's insistent coaching demands, Peter Kirkley, the talent scout, had urged Gazza: 'Be yourself, lad. Don't copy anybody.'

It was well-considered advice, generously given, and Gazza has never forgotten it. That's why you could almost feel his relief when he confirmed that his advisers were bringing a halt to Gazzamania. For it *was* beginning to change and restrict him: the carefree clown was becoming a furtive, distrusting recluse slightly afraid to say or do anything.

It is, of course, the media, not Gazza or his advisers, who will decide if so-called Gazzamania is over. The chances are that it won't be: popular newspapers adore a 'character'; and when that character is a lovable if mischievous imp and a footballing virtuoso with a charisma and magnetism to draw the crowds, then they will want to write about him. But Gazza has his feet on the ground and family and friends to help keep them there. In Terry Venables he has a boss who knows more than most how to enjoy life while working hard; who, as a motivator of people, is in a class of his own.

The boy who taught himself to play on the cobblestones of Gateshead now has the world at his talented feet; and what could lie ahead for him, and the millions who want to marvel at his magic, is quite breathtaking.

Don't bank on being a footballer, his teacher, Clive Hepworth, had told him. 'Only one in a thousand youngsters actually make it, you know.'

'Yes, I know,' said the boy. 'And that one will be me, sir!'

It was, Gazza, it was.

But with a difference: you're one in a million.

FOR THE BEST IN PAPERBACKS, LOOK FOR THE

In every corner of the world, on every subject under the sun, Penguin represents quality and variety – the very best in publishing today.

For complete information about books available from Penguin – including Puffins, Penguin Classics and Arkana – and how to order them, write to us at the appropriate address below. Please note that for copyright reasons the selection of books varies from country to country.

In the United Kingdom: Please write to *Dept E.P., Penguin Books Ltd, Harmondsworth, Middlesex, UB7 0DA.*

If you have any difficulty in obtaining a title, please send your order with the correct money, plus ten per cent for postage and packaging, to *PO Box No 11, West Drayton, Middlesex*

In the United States: Please write to *Dept BA, Penguin, 299 Murray Hill Parkway, East Rutherford, New Jersey 07073*

In Canada: Please write to *Penguin Books Canada Ltd, 2801 John Street, Markham, Ontario L3R 1B4*

In Australia: Please write to the *Marketing Department, Penguin Books Australia Ltd, P.O. Box 257, Ringwood, Victoria 3134*

In New Zealand: Please write to the *Marketing Department, Penguin Books (NZ) Ltd, Private Bag, Takapuna, Auckland 9*

In India: Please write to *Penguin Overseas Ltd, 706 Eros Apartments, 56 Nehru Place, New Delhi, 110019*

In the Netherlands: Please write to *Penguin Books Netherlands B.V., Postbus 195, NL–1380AD Weesp*

In West Germany: Please write to *Penguin Books Ltd, Friedrichstrasse 10–12, D–6000 Frankfurt/Main 1*

In Spain: Please write to *Longman Penguin España, Calle San Nicolas 15, E–28013 Madrid*

In Italy: Please write to *Penguin Italia s.r.l., Via Como 4, I-20096 Pioltello (Milano)*

In France: Please write to *Penguin Books Ltd, 39 Rue de Montmorency, F-75003 Paris*

In Japan: Please write to *Longman Penguin Japan Co Ltd, Yamaguchi Building, 2–12–9 Kanda Jimbocho, Chiyoda-Ku, Tokyo 101*

PENGUIN BESTSELLERS

The New Confessions William Boyd

The outrageous, hilarious autobiography of John James Todd, a Scotsman born in 1899 and one of the great self-appointed (and failed) geniuses of the twentieth century. 'Brilliant ... a Citizen Kane of a novel' – *Daily Telegraph*

The House of Stairs Barbara Vine

'A masterly and hypnotic synthesis of past, present and terrifying future ... compelling and disturbing' – *Sunday Times*. 'Not only ... a quietly smouldering suspense novel but also ... an accurately atmospheric portrayal of London in the heady '60s. Literally unputdownable' – *Time Out*

Summer's Lease John Mortimer

'It's high summer, high comedy too, when Molly drags her amiably bickering family to a rented Tuscan villa for the hols ... With a cosy fluency of wit, Mortimer charms us into his urbane tangle of clues...' – *Mail on Sunday*. 'Superb' – Ruth Rendell

Touch Elmore Leonard

'I bleed from five wounds and heal people, but I've never been in love. Isn't that something?' They call him Juvenal, and he's a wanted man in downtown Detroit... 'Discover Leonard for yourself – he's something else' – *Daily Mail*

Story of My Life Jay McInerney

'The first year I was in New York I didn't do anything but guys and blow...' 'The leader of the pack' – *Time Out*. 'Fast and sharp ... a very good novel indeed' – *Observer*

Riding the Iron Rooster   Paul Theroux

An eye-opening and entertaining account of travels in old and new China, from the author of *The Great Railway Bazaar*. 'Mr Theroux cannot write badly … in the course of a year there was almost no train in the vast Chinese rail network on which he did not travel' – Ludovic Kennedy

Touched by Angels   Derek Jameson

His greatest story yet – his own. 'My story is simple enough. I grew up poor and hungry on the streets of London's East End and decided at an early age it was better to be rich and successful.'

The Rich are Different   Susan Howatch

Wealth is power – and all power corrupts. 'A superb saga, with all the bestselling ingredients – love, hate, death, murder, and a hell of a lot of passion' – *Daily Mirror*

The Cold Moons   Aeron Clement

For a hundred generations the badgers of Cilgwyn had lived in harmony with nature – until a dying stranger limped into their midst, warning of the coming of men. Men whose scent had inexplicably terrified him, men armed with rifles and poison gas…

The Return of Heroic Failures   Stephen Pile

The runaway success of *The Book of Heroic Failures* was a severe embarrassment to its author. From the song-free Korean version of *The Sound of Music* to the least successful attempt to tranquillize an animal, his hilarious sequel plumbs new depths of human incompetence.

PENGUIN BESTSELLERS

A Sense of Guilt Andrea Newman

The sensational new novel by the author of *A Bouquet of Barbed Wire*. 'How pleasant life would be, he reflected, if he could have all three of them ... the virgin, the mother and the whore.' 'From the first toe-tingling sentence ... I couldn't put this bulky, breathless beanfeast of a novel down' – *Daily Mail*

Nice Work David Lodge

'The campus novel meets the industrial novel ... compulsive reading' – David Profumo in the *Daily Telegraph*. 'A work of immense intelligence, informative, disturbing and diverting ... one of the best novelists of his generation' – Anthony Burgess in the *Observer*

Difficulties With Girls Kingsley Amis

Last seen in *Take a Girl Like You*, Patrick Standish and Jenny, née Bunn, are now married and up-and-coming south of the Thames. Unfortunately, like his neighbours, Patrick continues to have difficulties with girls ... 'Very funny ... vintage Amis' – *Guardian*

The Looney Spike Milligan

Would Mick Looney's father lie on his HP deathbed? Well, he had to lie somewhere. When he told Mick that they are the descendants of the Kings of Ireland, was he telling the truth? If he was, why is Mick mixing cement in the rain in Kilburn? 'Hysterical' – *Time Out*

In the Midday Sun Guy Bellamy

On the sun-soaked Costa del Sol three fugitive brothers from England – bank robber, tax evader and layabout – contemplate the female form and the shape of things to come. But Matthew, Mark and Daniel have spent far too long in the midday sun ... 'The blue skies blacken very funnily indeed' – *Mail on Sunday*

FOR THE BEST IN PAPERBACKS, LOOK FOR THE 🐧

PENGUIN BESTSELLERS

Tomorrow is Too Late Ray Moore

With the wit and irreverence that made him famous, Ray Moore recalls the ups and downs of his broadcasting career and tells the heartwarming and intensely personal story of his fight for life – a story that is both an inspiration and a tribute to his immense courage.

Bad Girls, Good Women Rosie Thomas

In London, on the brink of the sixties, two runaways plunged into the whirl of Soho nightlife. They were raw and vulnerable – but both of them knew what they wanted from life. Mattie Banner and Julia Smith: together they broke all the rules.

Winner Maureen O'Donoghue

At fourteen, Macha Sheridan has nothing but her wagon, three unsaleable nags and one burning ambition – to breed a champion horse. It is an obsession that will take her from life among the Irish gypsies to the height of English society.

A Time and a Place Laura Gilmour Bennett

Cotton Castello, Prospero Vallone and Chiara Galla – the journalist, the magnate and the film star. Three lives enmeshed – at different times and in different places – in a web of passion, guilt and betrayal. Only now, at the Villa Robbiano, can the web be broken – and two lovers set free...

Unforgettable Fire: The Story of U2 Eamon Dunphy

The inside story of the rock phenomenon of the eighties. '*Unforgettable Fire* is a beacon ... in a cynical world' – *Time Out*

PENGUIN BESTSELLERS

Gorillas in the Mist Dian Fossey

For thirteen years Dian Fossey lived among the gorillas of the Virunga Mountains in Africa, defending them from brutal slaughter by poachers. In 1985 she was herself brutally murdered. *Gorillas in the Mist* is her story. 'Fascinating' – Paul Theroux

Presumed Innocent Scott Turow

The No. 1 International Bestseller. 'One of the most enthralling novels I have read in a long, long time' – Pat Conroy. 'If you start *Presumed Innocent* you will finish it … it grips like an octopus' – *Sunday Times*

The Second Rumpole Omnibus John Mortimer

Horace Rumpole turns down yet another invitation to exchange the joys and sorrows of life as an Old Bailey hack for the delights of the sunshine state and returns again in *Rumpole for the Defence*, *Rumpole and the Golden Thread* and *Rumpole's Last Case*.

Pearls Celia Brayfield

The Bourton sisters were beautiful. They were rich. They were famous. They were powerful. Then one morning they wake up to find a priceless pearl hidden under their pillows. Why? 'Readers will devour it' – *Independent*

Spring of the Ram Dorothy Dunnett
Volume 2 in the *House of Niccolò* series

Niccolò has now travelled as far as the frontier of Islam in order to establish the Silk Route for the Charetty empire. Beset by illness, feuds and the machinations of his rivals, he must use his most Machiavellian schemes to survive…

FOR THE BEST IN PAPERBACKS, LOOK FOR THE 🐧

BIOGRAPHY AND AUTOBIOGRAPHY IN PENGUIN

Just for William Nicholas Woolley and Sue Clayton

Originating as a film for the award-winning BBC2 documentary series *Forty Minutes*, *Just for William* is the story of William Clayton, diagnosed with leukaemia at the age of nine – and the story of a family who refused to give up hope in the battle against one of the deadliest diseases of all.

The Secret Lives of Trebitsch Lincoln Bernard Wasserstein

Trebitsch Lincoln was Member of Parliament, international spy, right-wing revolutionary, Buddhist monk – and this century's most extraordinary conman. 'An utterly improbable story … a biographical scoop' – *Guardian*

Tolstoy A. N. Wilson

'One of the best biographies of our century' – Leon Edel. 'All his skills as a writer, his fire as a critic, his insight as a novelist and his experience of life have come together in this subject' – Peter Levi in the *Independent*

Fox on the Run Graeme Fowler

The intimate diary of a dramatic eighteen months, in which Fowler became the first Englishman to score a double century in India – before being cast down by injury and forced to come to terms with loss of form. 'One of the finest cricket books this year' – *Yorkshire Post*. Winner of the first Observer/Running Late Sports Book Award.

Backcloth Dirk Bogarde

The final volume of Dirk Bogarde's autobiography is not about his acting years but about Dirk Bogarde the man and the people and events that have shaped his life and character. All are remembered with affection, nostalgia and characteristic perception and eloquence.

Jackdaw Cake Norman Lewis

From Carmarthen to Cuba, from Enfield to Algeria, Norman Lewis brilliantly recounts his transformation from stammering schoolboy to the man Auberon Waugh called 'the greatest travel writer alive, if not the greatest since Marco Polo'.